Pulling Together

PULLING TOGETHER

The Making of a Global Maritime Trade Union

ANDREW LININGTON

Whittles Publishing

Whittles Publishing Ltd.,
Dunbeath,
Caithness, KW6 6EG,
Scotland, UK

www.whittlespublishing.com

© 2023 Nautilus International
ISBN 978-184995-573-7

All rights reserved.
No part of this publication may be reproduced,
stored in a retrieval system, or transmitted,
in any form or by any means, electronic,
mechanical, recording or otherwise
without prior permission of the publishers.

Printed and bound in the UK
by Halstan Printing Group, Amersham

Contents

Foreword ix
Introduction xi

1 Coffin ships: roots of the union 1
2 'To promote the interests of the service':
    the launch of the MMSA 11
3 Welfare work: a legacy from the slave trade? 20
4 Rise of the guild: competition for the MMSA 23
5 Oil and water: the early engineers' union 36
6 Sparks fly: rise of the Radio Officers' Union 42
7 War and peace 1: birth of national negotiations 47
8 Unity at last: the Officers' Federation and the NEOU 56
9 Federation: a long-standing global vision 68
10 War and peace 2: building back better 75
11 Coming together: a single union for masters and officers 86
12 Going global: transition to a transboundary union 109
13 Going Dutch: uniting seafarers in the Netherlands 118
14 Swiss role: water work in a landlocked nation 128
15 Strength in unification: a union fit for the future 136

16   'A day that will live in infamy':

         P&O Ferries undermines recovery plans 141

17   Where to now? 149

     Addenda 155
     Notable figures 157
     Recurring themes 163
     What has the union ever done for us? 167
     List of abbreviations, initialisms and acronyms 175

Author's note

As this account inevitably contains numerous abbreviations, initialisms and acronyms, many of them historical, a list of them and their meanings appears at the end of the book.

Foreword

As the general secretary of the International Transport Workers' Federation (ITF), I have great pleasure in introducing the history of Nautilus International. This important organisation, one of our valued affiliates, is a true example of international solidarity in action. It has a proud history, as most eloquently portrayed in this book: a history of Nautilus intertwined with that of the ITF, and a history of its advocacy for maritime professionals, standing up for their rights and for the welfare of mariners in all sectors: seafaring, inland, and shore-based.

After the formation of Nautilus International in 2009, uniting Nautilus UK and Nautilus NL, it was joined in 2011 by maritime workers from Switzerland's Unia, enhancing international solidarity and cross-border cooperation yet further.

This book explains how Nautilus has been at the forefront of many campaigns that have shaped the maritime industry and improved the lives of transport workers. It is a strong advocate for fair pay and fair conditions, safety and security, training and education, social protection and environmental sustainability.

Nautilus is a key partner in the ITF's efforts to combat flags of convenience (FoC), to continually improve and enforce the Maritime Labour Convention (MLC), to protect seafarers' human rights, and to promote solidarity among maritime unions worldwide. Today it stands with us at the ITF in demanding a just transition as the global shipping industry wrestles with a necessarily ambitious environmental target to achieve net zero by 2050.

The strength of our partnership was evident during the crew change crisis brought about by the Covid pandemic. This left hundreds of thousands of seafarers stranded at sea for months beyond their contracts, unable to return home or even access medical care. This situation posed a serious threat to the human rights and the health and safety of seafarers, as well as to the functioning of global supply chains.

In response, Nautilus joined forces with the ITF, the International Labour Organization (ILO), the International Maritime Organization (IMO) and other stakeholders to advocate for seafarers to be designated as key workers. Thanks to this solidarity and cooperation, many governments adopted measures to facilitate crew changes and repatriation of seafarers during the pandemic, providing some relief to the maritime workforce. Nautilus International continues to work with its partners to ensure that seafarers are treated with dignity and respect.

This book tells the story of those achievements and the key challenges faced over the past decades, as well as Nautilus International's origins and evolution from its predecessor unions in the UK, the Netherlands and Switzerland. It is a tribute to the dedication and courage of the members, officers and staff who have made Nautilus a respected and influential voice in the maritime sector. It is also an inspiration for all transport workers who aspire to build a better future for themselves and their industry.

I congratulate Nautilus for all its achievements and its rich history – a proud history, a history underpinned by solidarity and commitment to international solidarity.

I am humbled to count so many of Nautilus' leaders, past and present, as good friends. I look forward to continuing our close collaboration in the years ahead.

Stephen Cotton
ITF General Secretary

Introduction

Shipmasters and officers might not spring to mind as workers in the vanguard of labour struggle. However, the evolution of a specialist trade union – ever at the cutting edge of deregulation and globalisation – to represent and protect the interests of its members, from distinguished masters to the rawest of recruits, serves up a story of immense interest, providing a pioneering model for the organisation of today's transnational economies.

Over the past two centuries the shipping industry worldwide has undergone extraordinary change, and within that change the seafaring profession has been radically reshaped. Sail to steam was just the start of an accelerating process of technological change which created new jobs, such as the marine engineer and the electro-technical officer, and made others, such as the radio officer, extinct. Transformation of models of ship ownership and operation, together with the rise of flags of convenience, helped to fuel further fundamental changes in the nature of seafaring and seafarers' relationships with their employers.

Organising members in such an environment has never been easy. Inherently isolated, often away from home for long periods and frequently pitted against each other, seafarers have always worked in conditions very different from those of employees ashore, and have often lacked the legal employment protections given to land-based workers.

Ever since vessels have been of a size to be crewed seafarers have also faced constant and unchanging challenges: the ever-present threats of unsafe ships and inaccurate navigation, the excessive (and disruptive) working hours and inadequate nutrition, and the risks of being replaced by lower-cost labour and of being treated as a criminal after making a mistake. These have all been depressingly recurring themes worldwide for centuries, and during the last two centuries, with the startling rise of global trade, they have become particularly apparent. Fortunately, in Britain the quest for fair treatment and a burning sense of injustice led in 1857 to the formation of the Mercantile Marine Service Association (MMSA) – the foundation stone in the building of today's union, Nautilus International.

Over the years of its evolution to its present transboundary status, the union has held true to its origins by promoting professional standards and certification while maintaining a constant commitment to the training and welfare of its members. From the provision of a much-needed training ship in 1859 to the development of specialist support services and state-of-the-art residential and care facilities for retired seafarers in the 21st century, the union has delivered far-reaching assistance for members at all stages of their careers.

Yet its history also shows that shipmasters and officers have not been afraid to deploy more traditional trade union tactics at crucial times. The engineer officers' dispute in 1914 assumed national significance, while action by the radio officers in 1920 secured increases that more than doubled their pre-war pay rates and sparked heated debates in Parliament. In more recent times, during the bleak years of the late 1970s and early 1980s strike action regularly served to head off the worst effects of flagging out and fleet cutbacks.

It was the prospect of industrial muscle flowing from collaboration between officers' and ratings' unions that in 1890 resulted in the decision by British shipowners to form the Shipping Federation as a 'fighting machine' to counter seafarer solidarity. However, the unions were to use a similar model to organise themselves in a novel and highly effective way. The creation of the Officers' (Merchant Navy) Federation in 1928 represented a radical move to foster unity across all the organisations representing masters and officers throughout the UK and the Commonwealth.

Internationalism had infused the British officers' organisations from their outset. In 1919, on the birth of the International Labour Organization (ILO), the MMSA, Imperial Merchant Service Guild (IMSG) and Marine Engineers' Association (MEA) worked with foreign unions, most notably their Dutch counterparts. From the first meeting of the ILO's Joint Maritime Commission in 1920, they pushed hard for action to tackle problems – problems which have nevertheless persisted to this day – such as long hours, sub-standard ships, and 'divide and rule' management techniques.

The international collaboration developed by the Officers' Federation percolated through to its decision to affiliate to the International Mercantile Marine Officers' Association (IMMOA) in 1936. Not only did the federation rapidly become a leading and galvanising force within IMMOA, but also it did much to broker its eventual affiliation to the International Transport Workers' Federation (ITF); and remarkably, some 70 years before the Maritime Labour Convention (MLC) came into being, it developed and promoted the concept of the International Seafarers' Charter, setting out detailed proposals for minimum standards and 'best practicable social legislation' for seafarers of all nationalities.

IMMOA also did much to promote deeper relationships between the Dutch and British unions, and it was with the eventual creation of Nautilus International in 2009 that the union formalised its cross-border status in a pioneering and radical response to what has been described as 'the negative consequences of globalisation and capital trans-nationalisation'. Together with its pivotal role in the development of the MLC, this transboundary tie-up delivered a strong symbol of the way in which the union remains determined to provide a powerful and effective voice for maritime professionals at a time of increasing consolidation amongst employers in the international shipping industry.

The launch of Nautilus International in 2009, bringing together British and Dutch unions, and the subsequent addition the Swiss union in 2011, demonstrated agility and the ability to respond to the constantly changing environment in which the organisation works. Whilst many of the challenges facing its members are seemingly perennial problems, the evolution of the union underlines its readiness to build on a proud past to confront the challenges of the future at a time when the shipping industry is once again on the brink of sweeping transformation.

1   COFFIN SHIPS:
ROOTS OF THE UNION

It's hard to think of any group of workers more in need of the support of a trade union than British merchant seafarers in the first half of the 19th century.

This was the era of the 'coffin ship', with horrifying accident rates; seafarers were six times more likely than coal miners, and 150 times more likely than factory workers, to be killed or injured at work. Added to that was the factor that while on average 3,360 seafarers died every year – 90 per cent of them as a consequence of drowning or disease – there was no system in place to recover the wages or effects of deceased seamen for their now desperate dependants.

In January 1843, during the space of just three days, 240 ships were wrecked and 500 lives lost, while between 1861 and 1870 there were more than 5,800

The scale of shipping losses in the early 19th century provoked public and political outrage. Around 450 people died when the steam clipper Royal Charter *was wrecked in a storm on the coast of Anglesey in 1859. The ship's loss led to the development of a weather forecasting service.*

shipwrecks, in which 8,105 lives were lost, around the British coastline. In 1834 Henry Woodruffe, secretary of the South Shields branch of the Seamen's Loyal Standard Association, told a Select Committee inquiry into the frequency of shipwrecks that in the previous four years one in four of all Tyne colliers had been lost.

At that time, too, there were no statutory provisions governing the supply of food or the accommodation of seafarers. Onboard conditions were often dire – damp and cramped, and lacking light and ventilation. Food was poor – usually a diet of dried and salted meat and brown biscuits or hard tack – and on foreign-going ships scurvy was common. Unsurprisingly, many seafarers were very sick men and often, by their forties, unable to continue working; cholera, dysentery, yellow fever, malaria and unspecified fevers were responsible for the deaths of thousands. It was suggested that only 1 in 200 would live long enough to be able to claim an early form of pension from the age of 60. And, as Richard Hope noted in his *History of British Shipping*, the mortality figures excluded those who went ashore to die.

Sir Gilbert Blane, the Scottish physician who had helped to radically improve health within the Royal Navy in the late 18th century, described merchant seafarers as having

> their constitutions worn out ten years before the rest of the laborious part of mankind. A seaman at the age of 45, if shewn to a person not accustomed to be among them, would be taken by his looks to be 55, or even on the borders of 60.

Not for nothing did the writer Samuel Johnson advise against sons being sent to sea:

> When you look down from the quarter deck to the space below, you see the utmost extremity of human misery; such crowding, such filth, such stench! No man will be a sailor who has contrivance enough to get himself into a jail; for being in a ship is being in a jail, with the chance of being drowned.

Prison, though, was also a constant threat for seafarers at this time. Any crew member daring to refuse to board a ship that they considered unseaworthy, overloaded or inadequately manned would be treated the same as deserters or drunkards who had failed to sail; they could face criminal prosecution and imprisonment with hard labour, typically for 12 weeks. In 1870 a total of 467 seamen were jailed for refusing to proceed to sea, and in 1854 prison inspectors in the south-west of England reported that 53 out of 239 men jailed during the past year had been seamen who had refused to sail because of unseaworthiness or undermanning.

Work at sea was not only dangerous, but also precarious. While in the early 19th century the British merchant fleet was the world's largest, frequent boom and bust cycles often triggered high rates of unemployment. Between 1815 and 1833 wages declined by around 40 per cent, with pay rates coming under pressure as the labour market was swamped by Royal Navy sailors no longer needed in the Napoleonic wars, which had ended. In addition, growing numbers of 'lascar'[1] seamen were employed from the mid-18th century, often at wages barely more than 15 per cent of European rates.

Things had become so bad that in 1788, when Parliament began to investigate the slave trade, the shocking evidence that emerged about the conditions for those captives aboard slave vessels meant diseases were common and made worse by over-crowding and poor ventilation below deck, leading to thousands of deaths. The conditions for crew were also poor. A House of Commons committee found that death rates among seafarers on Bristol and Liverpool slave ships were running at more than 21 per cent, and it has been estimated that between 1780 and 1807 more than 20,000 British slave-trade seafarers died.

Reformers such as William Wilberforce had been so concerned about the poverty and neglect faced by seafarers following the Napoleonic wars that in 1821 they helped to establish the Society for Distressed (Destitute) Seamen, which became the Seamen's Hospital Society.

There were no proper pensions for seafarers, no sick pay – and during their frequent spells of unemployment, no wages. The Merchant Seamen's Fund, an early form of a contributory pension scheme, had been established in 1747 to provide 'relief and support' for the many sick and disabled seafarers and the widows of those who had died at sea; but as the maritime workforce grew in the first half of the 19th century and shipowners cut their contributions, citing the need to compete with foreign operators, the increased demands made upon the fund meant that it struggled to cope. Between 1838 and 1845 seafarers repeatedly petitioned Parliament over its failure to provide adequate support, and their protests helped to secure a series of inquiries into the state of the fund. But the attempts made to secure its future through a form of tonnage tax or with state support failed; it was declared insolvent in 1849 and wound up in 1852 amid complaints of chronic mismanagement and misappropriation of its funds.

In the face of such appalling conditions, it is hardly surprising that seafarers became increasingly militant. From the 1730s onwards, protests over poor pay,

---

1 A term then used to describe crew members from India and China.

poor conditions and unemployment were staged in ports such as Sunderland, Southampton, Bristol, London and Liverpool, as well as demonstrations against the employment of 'foreigners' at lower wages. In May 1768 an estimated 14,000 seamen marched from Tower Hill to the Royal Exchange in support of petitions for improved pay and conditions, ahead of stoppages – which were then undermined by the deployment of the Royal Navy and the use of scab labour.

Between 1768 and 1854, crews of north-eastern coal trade ships – who amounted to an estimated 10 per cent of the mercantile marine workforce – repeatedly staged strike action, both over pay and conditions, and in opposition to the press gang system. In November 1792, there was a particularly successful stoppage by Tyneside collier crews in support of demands for extra pay during the arduous winter months. But in 1810 another strike, by Post Office packet crews in Falmouth protesting over poor pay and changes in working conditions, saw the local authorities reading the Riot Act, attempting to arrest the ringleaders and bringing in several Royal Navy ships to help move the Post Office vessels. In 1815 collier crews in the north-east of England organised further protests over poor pay and inadequate crewing scales, and even though the authorities once again called in the armed forces, the seafarers managed to win extra wages.

These latter protests took place at a time when trade union organisation was strictly prohibited by the Combination Acts of 1799 and 1800, which had introduced draconian penalties for any workers joining together to seek improved conditions such as an increase in wages or a decrease in hours.

Frederick Engels, writing in 1845, noted the additional problems that seafarers faced in trying to develop collective organisations: 'they cannot combine to raise wages because they are scattered, and if one alone refuses to work for low wages there are dozens out of work, or supported by the rates, who are thankful for the most trifling offer'.

However, some seafarers managed to develop collective organisations under the banner of friendly societies, such as the Sailors' Fund, founded in South Shields in 1798, the United Seamen's, Widows and Orphans Benefit Society, the Plimsoll British Seamen and Firemen's Defence Association, and the London Seamen's Mutual Protection Society, as well as the Seamen's Loyal Standard Association; this last, established following the repeal of the Combination Acts in 1824, is often considered to be the first seafarers' trade union.

These bodies followed a long tradition of mutual support amongst seafarers, which can be traced back to northern Europe of the Middle Ages. Fraternal bodies such as guilds, corporations and seamen's insurance boxes had been established in many maritime communities, usually serving to provide welfare support and relief, as well as to protect the interests of their members. They included societies such as the Seamen's Box of Aberdeen, founded in 1598 (later to become the Aberdeen Shipmaster Society), to make provision for the families of masters and mariners drowned at sea.

Shipmasters' societies, which began to emerge in the mid-18th century, also acted as a form of mutual support, providing pensions and other assistance to members and their families, as well as working to raise the professional status of seafarers and supporting the creation of schools of navigation. Master mariners' associations in Newcastle and Shields helped to establish homes for 'worn-out' members in the 1830s, and ran a mutual scheme of insurance for personal effects.

Although most of these organisations had, on the surface at least, been created to provide some sort of pension or welfare provision, many became effective lobbying organisations, and they presented compelling evidence on behalf of seafarers to politicians and Parliament.

In 1833 a petition presented by the 'Officers and Sailors of the Commercial Navy of the Kingdom' urged the House to consider whether 'some well digested, printed and generally circulated, code of laws for Merchant Shipping' should be established; another petition, submitted in the same year by 1,100 'Friends of the British Sea Service', urged Parliament to establish a general maritime code of laws for the regulation of the mercantile marine and the provision of facilities to support seafarers in old age or following accidents at sea.

When, a decade or two earlier, seafarers had begun to make collective representations to government, they had helped to focus mounting public and political unease about the scale of death and injury, and the abysmal conditions, at sea. In turn, this resulted in a series of regulatory initiatives that sought to address some of the worst problems; 1819 saw an Act 'for facilitating the Recovery of the Wages of Seamen in the Merchant Service', which reduced the waiting time for final pay-off, and in 1823 there was an early attempt to build the British maritime skills base with the introduction of regulations requiring that all merchant ships of 80 tons or more should carry apprentices, according to a tonnage-based scale – a principle that Nautilus sought to uphold two centuries later.

The Merchant Shipping Act of 1835 consolidated regulations governing merchant seafarers introduced in the previous century and sought to bring greater government scrutiny over shipping and seafaring; as well as introducing requirements for British-registered ships to carry crew agreements and accounts, it established the Registrar and Register Office of Merchant Seamen to record the service of all British seafarers and provide an early form of database to help crew Royal Navy ships in times of war.

The responsibility for merchant shipping within government had been fragmented between nine different departments, including the Admiralty and the Colonial Office, none of which had the absolute authority for the direction and supervision of mercantile policy. However when the Board of Trade was created in 1786 and gradually took over the 'general Superintendence of Matters relating to the British Mercantile Marine', things began to change.

As part of its efforts to improve safety at sea, the Board of Trade became increasingly concerned with the need to raise the standards of seafarers. Political pressure had intensified in the first half of the 19th century following a succession of reports from British diplomats complaining about the poor quality of British crews. In 1834 James Buchanan, HM Consul in New York, wrote to the Foreign Office to warn that unless measures were taken to regulate British shipping and to employ 'competent persons', American vessels would soon dominate the growing transatlantic passenger trade. In the same year, the influential *Edinburgh Review* suggested that nearly half the losses at sea were the consequence of incompetence and carelessness in masters.

In 1843 Henry Plaw, the British consul in Danzig,[2] wrote: 'Taken as a whole, there is not – and I say it with regret – a more troublesome and thoughtless set of men, to use the mildest term, to be met with than British merchant seamen.' And William Hertslet, the vice-consul in Memel,[3] warned that the 'heedless conduct' of officers and seamen was giving British shipping a very bad name.

In response to these repeated accounts of poorly trained and poorly behaved crews in foreign ports, which had been collated in a memorandum to Parliamentary Under-Secretary of State for Foreign Affairs Lord Canning in 1843, the Foreign Office began to demand action.

Many seafarers, too, had been actively pressing for improvements. Back in 1836, for example, a petition from the masters, mates and seamen of Kirkcaldy had highlighted the need for a system 'similar to the practice for officers of the Royal Navy, and formerly for officers of the East India Company's naval service, for pilots and for many professions ashore'. A couple of years before that, seamen in South Shields had voiced their concerns about the lack of any inquiry into the circumstances of ship losses, and had advocated the establishment of a nautical committee both to enquire into the construction and provisioning of merchant vessels – and, courageously, to examine the 'abilities and conduct of the commanders and officers'.

The 1836 Report of the Select Committee on Shipwrecks, commissioned in response to the loss of 1,702 ships over a three-year period, concluded that it had indeed been the incompetence of masters and officers that was one of the prime causes of the lamentable safety record. It found evidence that many masters and

---
2 Then in Prussia, now Gdansk in Poland
3 Then in Prussia, now Klaipeda in Lithuania

officers were unable to navigate properly, read charts or follow courses. In 1834 one Captain Henry Hyland had told the annual dinner of the Royal Humane Society that a great number of his fellow masters and mates were 'entirely ignorant of the use of a sextant or chronometer'.

Hardly surprising, when the Select Committee was also told of masters being frequently appointed to command despite little seagoing experience. George Coleman, a teacher of navigation, gave evidence that the 279-ton ship *Headleys* on the Belfast–Quebec run had been commanded by a 14-year-old boy, while another witness testified that a warehouse porter had been selected by owners to command a seagoing ship. The report also noted that drunkenness was 'a frequent cause of ships being wrecked' and that it often resulted in 'improper and contradictory orders and directions on the part of the officers' and 'sleeping on the look-out or at the helm among the men'.

The committee produced a set of recommendations for improving the construction, equipment and navigation of merchant vessels. Its members argued that the merchant marine should be professionalised, and they put forward proposals which, they hoped, would 'elevate and improve the general character of the British Mercantile Marine' and 'make its officers the most distinguished for their competency and skill'. As well as proposing the creation of a Mercantile Marine Board to 'direct, superintend and regulate all shipping affairs', they recommended the establishment of nautical schools, a system to examine officers for competency in seamanship, navigation and nautical astronomy, and to institute courts of inquiry into all cases of shipwreck.

However, the government, not persuaded by the committee's findings, said that further evidence was needed to justify the introduction of new regulations. Committee chairman James Silk Buckingham, a former seafarer who had campaigned strongly against the practice of impressment and the hated press gangs, introduced a Private Member's Bill that sought to implement the recommendations – but at its second reading it was soundly defeated. Among its opponents was the President of the Board of Trade, Poulett Thomson, who argued that the introduction of compulsory examinations for British shipmasters would amount to an 'unjust interference with the shipping interest'.

By that point, however, the pressure for action was becoming hard to resist. Whilst the main owners' organisation, the General Shipowners' Society, veered between outright hostility and indifference to the proposals for examinations and certification, a group of Scottish owners had campaigned strongly for them, and operators such as the East India Company and the Royal Mail Line were already making successful use of their own systems to test the competence of their masters and officers.

In 1842 Vice-Admiral Robert Fitzroy led an early, but unsuccessful, bid to introduce certification for merchant seafarers.

Vice-Admiral Robert Fitzroy, who became a Tory MP after commanding Darwin's ship, HMS *Beagle*, took up the fight, and in 1842 led a deputation of MPs to meet the President of the Board of Trade, the Earl of Ripon, to call for the certification of ships' officers. Subsequently, Fitzroy introduced a Bill for the improvement of conditions in the Merchant Navy, but it was unsuccessful. He countered the free trade argument by pointing out that some companies were choosing to send their cargoes in foreign ships because of the poor standards of British vessels and their crews.

With more horrifying losses at sea, a second Select Committee hearing into the frequency of shipwrecks was established in 1843. It heard that many 'competitor' countries, such as France, the Netherlands, Denmark, Sweden and Russia, had implemented systems for testing and certifying their masters and officers, together with a code of laws regulating the conduct and competency of their officers. It recommended not only the introduction of a system to examine the ability, conduct and character of those seeking to qualify as masters and mates but also the establishment of navigation schools, funded by a tonnage-based levy on ships.

Two years later the Board of Trade finally agreed to the introduction of voluntary certificates for masters and mates, with examinations conducted by local boards and overseen by Trinity House. However, faced with evidence showing that the scheme was extraordinarily ineffectual – with only 131 masters and 35 mates sitting these examinations in its first year of operation, and a total of just 1,239 certificates being awarded in the first three years – it was forced to take more effective action.

While successive governments had increasingly regulated certain aspects of the shipping industry, the spirit of free trade had generated somewhat conflicting moves to relax the long-standing controls over the flags and crews of ships carrying cargoes into, out of and around the UK. This resulted in a decision in 1847 to establish a Select Committee inquiry into 'the operation and policy of the Navigation Laws'. Although much of the evidence examined the workings of the protectionist measures, a considerable amount of time was spent discussing the demands to improve the quality of British seafarers – especially in the face of fresh evidence, provided by the Foreign Office, of poor standards of competence and conduct. As a consequence, proposals for a Navigation Bill, announced in February 1849, stated: 'it is expedient to remove the restrictions which prevent the free carriage of goods by sea to and from the United Kingdom and the British Possessions abroad' and to 'amend the Laws for the Registration of Ships and Seamen'.

Once the Navigation Bill had been passed, in June 1849, the government announced further plans to 'improve the condition of Masters, Mates and Seamen in the Merchant Service' – including the introduction of compulsory examinations for masters and mates. As the Registrar General of Seamen had argued, these were necessary not only to ensure that those in charge of life and property should possess appropriate qualifications, 'but in order the better to enable Masters of British vessels to compete with foreigners for freights in the markets of the world, by the production of satisfactory credentials as to their competency'.

Next, the Mercantile Marine Act, passed in August 1850 despite a concerted campaign from hostile shipowners, set out a system of compulsory examinations for masters and mates in the foreign-going trades, and outlined the qualifications and experience required for the award of certificates for masters, first mates, 'only mates' and second mates, as well as the syllabus for an extra master's certificate 'for persons desirous of obtaining the command of ships and steamers of the first class'. The Act also established local marine boards with the duties of examining masters and mates and issuing certificates of competency. The boards were also given the power to initiate investigations into complaints about the moral and professional misconduct of masters and officers, with the Board of Trade having the sole right to formally suspend or cancel a certificate of competency.

Despite the fact that many seafarers had called for the introduction of examinations and certification, the 1850 Act generated a very negative response, with complainants describing its provisions as 'tyrannous'. The concomitant introduction of 22 new disciplinary offences and procedures for seamen, along with requirements for the men to make payments to the local shipping offices whenever they signed on or off ships, led to local strikes and other protests. This in turn led to the formation of the Seamen's United Protection Society, known as the Penny Union, which lobbied MPs and the Board of Trade, and had some success in securing concessions to the fees system and suspension of the disciplinary offences.

The Act also spurred the formation of the British Mariners' Association, established in February 1851 at a public meeting held in Liverpool. The association sought to defend the interests and the rights of masters, officers and seamen, claiming to be 'the only constitutional means of obtaining from Parliament such practical, reasonable, and efficient laws for the merchant service of this country'. The inaugural meeting expressed opposition to the 'obnoxious clauses' within the 1850 Act, and its 'arbitrary and oppressive' implications for seafarers. The association also took exception to the new disciplinary measures, and stood against the repeal of the Navigation Laws as well as calling for experienced masters to be exempt from the new examinations – but its existence was short-lived; it appears not to have survived beyond 1852.

Another sign of the growing unhappiness of shipmasters and officers came in a letter to the *Shipping & Mercantile Gazette* in April 1844. The writer, signing off as 'British Shipmaster', complained about 'the inefficiency of the law for the protection of the masters and crews of merchant ships', and the fact that 'the members of every other profession or calling are protected, while we appear to be outcasts from the rest of society through our isolated position'. Consequently, he argued, a shipmaster was 'not paid more than a boy in a broker's office, because he has to compete with the foreigner', and the creation of a union was both 'necessary and desirable … in order to obtain laws for our mutual welfare'.

Such sentiments were to grow as the government pressed on with its programme to reform the shipping industry. MPs had heard complaints about the lack of adequate investigations into maritime accidents, with some blaming the high rate of incidents on a lack of accountability and responsibility among shipmasters and arguing that 'the imperfectly defined power of masters and frequent ignorance as to the extent of authority causes extremes of leniency and tyranny'. The 1854 Merchant Shipping Act therefore took the investigative and disciplinary process further, amplifying the provisions of the 1850 Act, and ending the traditional status of the masters as 'second unto God' on their ships by making them answerable not just to the owners but also to the state. It was a fundamental change – one that provided the catalyst for the creation of a new organisation dedicated to the best interests of the 'Officers of the Mercantile Marine of the United Kingdom'…

2 'To promote the interests of the service': the launch of the MMSA

On Friday 3 April 1857 a 'very numerous attendance' of shipmasters, officers and owners met in Liverpool's Cotton Sale Room to consider the 'arbitrary and oppressive powers' introduced by the Merchant Shipping Act just three years earlier. Section 8 of the 1854 Act, covering inquiries into wrecks and casualties at sea, had introduced a controversial tribunal system which one speaker at the meeting described as 'a gross injustice'.

Masters and officers considered that the courts of inquiry were impartial and 'incompetent through ignorance', with insufficient nautical expertise on the panels, and that they handed out excessively harsh penalties. Not only that, but masters and officers were denied the right of appeal against the findings.

Such a state of affairs, Captain Henry Ward (later to become MMSA president) told the inaugural meeting, was a national disgrace and meant that the system did not allow shipmasters and officers the privileges given to criminals.

The meeting, which had been organised by local shipowner Ralph Brocklebank and Captain Charles Judkins of Cunard's American Royal Mail

Captain Charles Judkins, master of the Cunard ship Persia, *jointly organised the April 1857 meeting in Liverpool, which unanimously agreed to establish the Mercantile Marine Service Association.*

Service, adopted two resolutions: one condemning the 'unjust' workings of the tribunals, and the other calling for the merchant service to be given a process in line with that of the Royal Navy, with charges to be considered by a 'tribunal of their own class'. It was agreed that both these resolutions should be carried forward in a petition to Parliament.

But the meeting went much further than simple opposition to the tribunal system, with a succession of speakers talking about the 'moral and intellectual advance' of the men of the merchant service and of the need for 'a large and powerful body' to protect their interests. Those present unanimously approved a resolution calling for the formation of such a body – the Mercantile Marine Service Association – with the core aim of taking 'every legitimate step to elevate to their proper position the officers of the mercantile marine of the United Kingdom'.

Introducing this motion, Captain James Atkins commented: 'There was a time when the sailors of our country were looked upon as a superstitious set of beings who thought of nothing but his love for sweethearts and tobacco.' Now, however, shipmasters and officers were determined to demonstrate that they were 'members of a profession at once honourable and enlightened'.

Atkins appealed to those present at the meeting to support the establishment of the association. 'The profession demands it,' he added, 'and when the master mariner is absent from the shores of Old England, he will feel that his interests are being attended to, even in his absence, by those at home.'

Within a fortnight, the MMSA moved into temporary offices in Chapel Street, and its 40-member executive council published an appeal for all masters and officers of the mercantile marine service to join it, and support its aims and objectives. The association rapidly set to work to address the ills identified in the founding meeting, and at the end of April it held another meeting to start a petition to Parliament against the 'arbitrary powers' exercised by the Board of Trade as it investigated the causes of wrecks. It also agreed plans to address 'one of the greatest wants in the port of Liverpool' by opening a reading room for members to which 'nautical men could resort to obtain information, to pass their time, and to transact their business'. Once opened, the rooms provided books in which masters, officers and engineers 'desirous to obtain appointments' could add their names, and within a year the MMSA reported that this service was being used 'to a very considerable extent' by shipowners seeking seagoing staff.

In February 1858 the MMSA organised another meeting in the Cotton Sale Room, chaired by the Mayor of Liverpool, to consider proposals for amendments to the 1854 Act to ensure the presence of experienced shipmasters on local marine boards hearing nautical cases. In an uncanny precursor to future campaigns against the criminalisation of seafarers more than 150 years later, Captain James Anderson seconded the motion by complaining about seafarers being 'tried almost as a criminal for what was merely, generally speaking, an error of judgement'. The same meeting also discussed concerns about the welfare of 'sick, worn out, and disabled' seafarers, and ways in which the men of the mercantile marine could be given 'the same standing as other professions'.

It then approved the text of a petition to the Queen, seeking a charter of incorporation for the MMSA; the charter was granted in 1863 through a special Act of Parliament. The petition had noted that 'Officers, possessing all the requisite qualities, abound in the merchant service; but as they have no means of acting in concert, the profession generally derives but little benefit from their influence or example'. The MMSA, it promised, would not only seek to advance the interests of the officers and men of the merchant service, but also provide 'refuges and hospitals for aged, sick and worn out' seafarers and 'establish schools afloat and on shore for the education and training of boys and men for the service'.

Acting with impressive speed, the association's council had intensely lobbied Royal Navy interests for a couple of cadet ships, and managed within the space of just two years to secure the loan of HMS *Conway*, a 26-year-old 28-gun frigate, from the Admiralty. The MMSA raised £1,200[4] to have the ship re-rigged and re-fitted as a school 'for the better training and educating of boys wishing to enter and prosper in the mercantile marine service'. It was moored off Rock Ferry, Birkenhead, and was given the role of instructing its 120 residents in practical seamanship navigation. The MMSA Council expressed the hope that those passing through its classes would 'become in future years known as the foremost among our merchant officers for their intelligence, intrepidity, and knowledge of seamanship'.

Conway quickly proved such a success that in 1861 a larger vessel, the 51-gun frigate *Winchester*, had to be requisitioned from the Admiralty. The school flourished further, and in 1875 the Admiralty offered the battleship *Nile* as an even larger facility. Over the following 99 years, including the final 21 as a shore-based establishment, *Conway* made a major contribution to UK maritime training, and its 11,500-plus cadets were highly valued by the industry and the Royal Navy. Its alumni included not only notable figures such as Poet Laureate John Masefield, but also the founder of the Navigators' & Engineer Officers' Union, William Coombs; the Merchant Navy and Airline Officers' Association general secretary, Eric Nevin; and the National Union of Marine, Aviation and Shipping Transport Officers (NUMAST) deputy general secretary, Derek Bond.

---

4 Equivalent in early 2023 to ~£193,000

Above: HMS Conway *cadets in the 1880s. More than 11,500 seafarers were trained by the 'school ship' until its closure in 1974.*

Left: The training ship HMS Conway *was up and running within two years of the creation of the MMSA as part of its drive to improve standards of seamanship.*

Another early win for the MMSA was the Admiralty's approval in 1861 of regulations to enable 'commanders and officers of the Merchant Service' to be granted commissions in the Royal Naval Reserve, which had been established in 1859.

Within the space of two years, MMSA membership rose to more than 1,000, and it dropped the words 'of Liverpool and the Western Ports' from its title as a sign of its intentions to organise on a wider basis, following a fairly acrimonious dispute with the London shipmasters' body. The discontent amongst seafarers had seen similar associations, sharing many of the same aims, established in a number of major ports; in June 1857 some of the Liverpool MMSA Council members had helped to set up the London MMSA. However, there was a distinct difference of opinion over the extent to which they should work with shipowners and merchants to tackle the problems which had been identified. Despite the divisions, Liverpool MMSA sought to unite all the associations in petitioning on behalf of the profession, and it acted quickly, establishing within its first year a formal presence in the ports of Dublin, Cork, Belfast, Fleetwood and Whitehaven.

Speaking at the MMSA's third annual meeting, Mr Samuel Graves (later to become the MP for Liverpool) stated:

> If we consider how difficult it is for individuals, however just their grievances may be, to make themselves heard in this community … I feel satisfied that the advantages of this Association will become so apparent and so essential that instead of having a thousand members,

either this or other kindred associations throughout the Kingdom will number every officer of the Mercantile Marine in England. It is only by some such combined action as that, that you can make your voices heard and have your wants redressed.

The welfare of members was high on the agenda from the outset, and the MMSA Council moved quickly to establish a Benevolent and Provident Fund, designed to provide members with an annuity of £20 per annum, and relief for members, widows and children 'in distress and sudden calamity'.

The 1863 annual meeting heard a call for an end to the 'fearful' system of crimping: predatory agents would manage seamen's wages and, through bribery and coercion, encourage them to desert, then supply their bereft ships with new crewmen, for a commission. Associate member Christopher Bushell told the meeting that 'shipmasters were no doubt as much accustomed to encounter this evil as that the tide of the Mersey will ebb and flow', and argued that a river police force was required to eradicate the practice. The MMSA Council followed this up with the Mersey Docks and Harbour Board, and within the space of a year was able to report that 'measures are in progress for the suppression of the nefarious traffic which exists'.

As the 1862 Merchant Shipping Act failed to include any amendments to the hated system of inquiries into shipping casualties, the MMSA petitioned Parliament in 1864, and took part in a deputation to the Board of Trade to protest at the 'anomalous, unconstitutional and un-English nature' of the tribunals. In 1870, in complaints about ministerial turnover that continue to resonate today, the MMSA reported: 'Perhaps nothing can more effectually account for this constant disappointment, owing to nothing being done, than the changes so frequently taking place in the Board of Trade department.'

The association had highlighted a series of cases in which, it argued, shipmasters had been unjustly penalised by having their certificate withdrawn or suspended following an inquiry. It made repeated representations to have sentences commuted or reversed, and was particularly outraged by the case of Captain James Fisher, whose certificate was suspended after his ship, *Dunmail*, was wrecked at the mouth of the Mersey while under compulsory pilotage. In a letter to the Board of Trade, Captain Ward questioned the logic of holding the master liable for the ship's loss when the pilot had been on board, 'because the law presumed that his knowledge of local dangers was superior to the master's'.

In another case, which it described as 'an outrageous injustice', the MMSA was in the forefront of protests when a member, Captain Charles Barnes, was jailed after being found guilty of 'illegally imprisoning' a seaman in leg irons for failing to obey orders. Barnes, master of the Hall Line clipper *Locksley Hall*, had ordered that the man, William Allen, should be kept in chains until the ship arrived in London at the end of a voyage from Australia. Allen was brought before the Thames Police Court and charged with wilful neglect of duty and assaulting the ship's chief mate. However, the magistrate – stating that Allen had been 'cruelly treated' – imposed a nominal sentence of just two days' imprisonment. He then heard Allen's counter-summons of assault by Captain Barnes, and sentenced the master to 21 days in prison.

The case sparked outrage, with claims of a serious miscarriage of justice and warnings of a breakdown in shipboard discipline. More than 400 shipmasters, owners and marine insurers signed a joint statement of protest; questions were raised in Parliament and representations made to the home secretary and the prime minister. The MMSA declared that unless Captain Barnes was immediately released, 'recourse must be had to such measures as would move the whole maritime interest of the country'. Faced by the storm of protest, the home secretary announced that it had been decided to remit the remainder of the sentence given to Captain Barnes, and he was released after serving just seven days.

However, the frustrating lack of progress on the core aim of changing the inquiry system, combined with a downturn in the shipping industry, was cited as the cause of a dip in MMSA membership at the start of the 1870s. President Captain Henry Ward said it was unfair to blame the association for the failure of politicians, and complained that it was 'really surprising to find how great was the ignorance which prevailed as to the actual work done'.

In 1873 the association wrote to the Royal Commission, investigating shipping safety and considering Samuel Plimsoll's proposals for ships to undergo regular surveys. It called for the inquiry to be widened to include 'the present deteriorated condition, professionally, of our seamen' and the damage caused by the abolition in 1854 of the compulsory apprenticeship system. 'A very large proportion of all the casualties that occur at sea are preventable and are partly owing to the want of training and discipline in our seamen,' stated Captain Ward.

The 1854 Merchant Shipping Act had also abolished the historic Navigation Act provisions requiring at least three-quarters of the crew of British ships to be British seafarers. This move, justified on the grounds of opening up free trade, saw the number of foreign seafarers on British ships rise from 7,321 to 13,230 within the space of just one year. In another taste of things to come, the MMSA had expressed its concern about the Board of Trade granting certificates to 'Foreigners, especially Americans' to enable them to command and to navigate British ships. The MMSA Council warned that this would 'act injuriously in preventing a respectable class of young men from entering the Service with the view to attain the rank of officers in it, on account of the low rate of remuneration which Foreigners will accept'.

Not only was the MMSA continuing to lobby Parliament for changes to the casualty inquiry system, but it was also actively seeking to 'raise the position of the merchant officers'. In furthering its founding aim to 'promote the improvement of nautical knowledge', the association was claiming within a couple of years to have helped 'many hundreds of Masters or Officers' to secure jobs at sea, and also asserting that its reading and newsrooms, opened at its offices in Water Street, Liverpool, had contributed to the 'social elevation of members'. It had in addition campaigned to have the electoral franchise extended to certificated masters of the merchant service.

The association was part of a broader movement to end the practice of crimping, and had also highlighted a range of health and safety problems, including the poor quality of food on many ships, as well as concerns that the chronic prevalence of scurvy amongst merchant seafarers was linked to the sub-standard supplies of lime juice sent to many vessels.

In response to a rise in shipping accidents (from 1,667 casualties and losses in 1860 to 2,289 in 1866), the MMSA pressed for more lightships in the Irish Sea, more storm signals, improved ship surveying and better compass adjusting. It helped to secure the appointment of a special committee of the House of Lords to investigate concerns about the unsatisfactory ballasting of merchant ships, and also sought improvements in the standard of shipboard accommodation, better controls over the carriage of dangerous deck cargoes in winter, and measures to tackle the navigation of large vessels by uncertificated officers.

The MMSA was from the outset highly attuned to the special welfare needs of seafarers and their families, and it played a crucial role in the creation of a Liverpool home to care for the orphans of merchant seafarers. On 16 December 1868 a public meeting convened at the MMSA Rooms agreed a resolution to found 'an establishment for feeding, clothing and educating the fatherless children of seamen'. Within the space of eight months sufficient money had been raised to open a temporary home for 46 boys and 14 girls. In April 1870 Liverpool Town Council agreed to provide a site by Newsham Park for the construction of the Seamen's Orphan Institution. This was formally opened on 30 September 1874 by the Duke of Edinburgh – Queen Victoria's second son, the 'sailor prince' – who had in 1861 accepted an offer of honorary membership of the MMSA Council. By the end of the century it was housing more than 320 children and providing assistance to a further 500-plus. The orphanage continued to operate until 1949, and the institution remains one of the UK's largest grant-givers for families who have lost a seafaring parent.

Concerns over the often desperate circumstances facing seafarers when they came ashore resulted in an early move by the MMSA to remodel its welfare activities, with a commitment to provide 'a home and maintenance for friendless, single, aged, incapacitated mariners; cottage homes for aged mariners, and their wives; and pensions or relief for aged mariners, their widows and children'. This led to the launch in 1870 of The Aged Seamen's Annuity and Widows' Casual Relief Fund, to provide grants and small pensions. Among the first to be assisted by the fund was Captain John Oliver, who had spent 70 years working at sea, including serving with Nelson at Trafalgar, and had commanded a ship at the age of 86. He went on to live to the age of 102.

The association also pressed ahead with the creation of a fund for building a home for 'decayed merchant seamen'. The idea of such facilities did not meet with universal approval; Liverpool MP John Torr told the 1874 general meeting that 'the idea of these dwellings of charity originates from the workhouse, and the asylum' and that it would 'simply stamp so many recipients of our bounty as comparative paupers'.

However, to support its campaign to make better welfare provision for 'ancient mariners', the MMSA had emphasised the fact that many thousands of former seafarers were ending up in poorhouses. Within the space of five years its appeal had raised more than £12,000,[5] and in October 1882 the foundation stone was laid for the main building in the new Liverpool Homes for Aged Mariners. Built with the support of the merchant and benefactor William Cliff, it housed 65 men, and in the following 95 years of its operation it accommodated a total of 1,113 residents. The original facilities, which also included two cottage homes that had been completed earlier in the year, were formally opened in December 1882 by the Duke of Edinburgh.

The homes were built in a 5-acre site on the banks of the Mersey; the plot had been donated by the estate of Roger Lyon Jones, a former Liverpool City Councillor. By the turn of the 20th century the MMSA had managed to acquire further land to enable more houses, an infirmary and a home for widows to be built on what became known as the Mariners' Park Estate. All this laid the foundations for a unique and specialist set of welfare facilities which evolved and expanded in the following decades under the supervision of the welfare branch committee; it also managed various charitable and pension funds, and until 1968 had responsibility for the MMSA's educational and training work through HMS *Conway*.

---

5 Equivalent in early 2023 to well over £1.8 million.

PROPOSED HOMES FOR AGED MARINERS
'WHO HAVE SAILED OUT OF LIVERPOOL AS MASTERS OR OFFICERS IN THE BRITISH MERCHANT SERVICE; PREFERENCE BEING GIVEN TO ELIGIBLE CANDIDATES WHO HAVE BEEN MEMBERS OF THE MERCANTILE MARINE SERVICE ASSOCIATION.'

Above: Original plans for the 'refuges for aged, sick and worn-out officers of the Mercantile Marine' which were formally opened by the Duke of Edinburgh – an honorary member of the MMSA Council – in December 1882.

Left: Some of the first residents at the Liverpool Home for Aged Mariners.

Lower: The MMSA launched a major fund-raising campaign which resulted in the opening of a home for seafarers' widows in 1906.

3   Welfare work: a legacy from the slave trade?

By the end of the 18th century Liverpool had become one of the world's biggest slave-trading ports – so it may come as no surprise (albeit a very uncomfortable thought) to learn of the links between the barbaric business and the origins of the union's Merseyside welfare work for seafarers.

Although 50 years had elapsed between the official end of the British slave trade and the launch of the MMSA, its legacy lingered in that many of the former slave-ship merchants simply switched their cargoes to raw materials imported from countries where slave labour continued.

British ships had been involved in the slave trade since the 1560s, and by the 1740s Liverpool had overtaken Bristol to become the biggest British slaving port, in terms of both the number of ships sailing to Africa and the number of slaves carried across the Atlantic. It has been estimated that Liverpool ships transported more than 1.1 million slaves; at one stage the port's ships had a share amounting to almost 80 per cent of the British slave trade and 40 per cent of the European trade.

Conditions on the slave ships were appalling, and at one stage around 25 per cent of the captives died during the voyages. A diagram of the Liverpool slave ship *Brookes*, showing the vessel crammed with 454 people, proved highly effective in raising awareness of the awful reality of the trade. However, *Brookes* had actually been carrying as many as 609 slaves at a time until the Regulated Slave Trade Act of 1788 sought to control conditions on board British slave ships, limiting the numbers that could be transported and requiring the carriage of qualified surgeons. The sickness and death rates among the ships' crews were also appalling; because the tween decks were used to hold the human cargoes many seafarers had to sleep on deck, and large numbers fell victim to infections such as malaria and yellow fever.

While there were many appalling accounts of brutality among the slave ship crews, some of the seamen were so horrified by their experiences that they became key figures in the abolition movement. John Newton, for example, who had been a master of slave ships before he renounced his role in the business, became a clergyman and worked closely with William Wilberforce on the abolition campaign. Edward Rushton served as an officer on Liverpool slave ships and also became a leading abolitionist as a result of his time in the trade. After losing much of his eyesight when he contracted ophthalmia on one voyage, he went on to establish a school for the blind in Liverpool.

The 1807 Abolition of Slavery Act finally put an official end to the British trade – though not without some opposition. Liverpool MP Isaac Gascoyne, for instance, argued in the House of Commons that ending the business would put 4,000 seafarer jobs and 40,000 tons of British shipping at risk. In reality, however, although Liverpool had by that time become by far the biggest British slave trade port, its ships had increasingly diversified into other operations. It has been estimated that between 1792 and 1807 the proportion of the Liverpool-registered fleet running slave voyages fell from just over 8 per cent to barely 4 per cent.

But the slave trade had laid the foundations for the city's expansion, its prosperity, and its longer-term trade and development. Many of the merchants and shipowners who became wealthy on the back of the business had, as intimated above, simply converted their vessels to carry raw materials such as palm oil, sugar and cotton, and Liverpool continued to dominate the West African trades for decades to follow.

The huge scale of the Liverpool slave trade meant that a number of the owners and merchants supporting the MMSA's welfare work or serving as honorary or associate members, including families such as the Tobins, Horsfalls, Gladstones and Brocklebanks, had direct or indirect connections to the business. However, the honorary MMSA members also included some with links to the abolition movement, such as the Rathbone Brothers, Quaker timber merchants.

A connection to the slave trade is also evident in the foundation of Mariners' Park. The money to build what was initially known as The Liverpool Home for Aged Mariners had come from William Cliff, the son of the Liverpool merchant Adam Cliff, who was part owner of a plantation in Jamaica.

A plaque to commemorate the opening of Cliff House in 1882 clearly sought to portray Adam Cliff in a favourable light, stating that

> although against his own interest as a Jamaica merchant, he was always a strong advocate for the suppression of slavery in our West India colonies then cultivated by slave labour, and warmly sympathised with all measures for ameliorating the wants and sufferings of his fellow creatures.

Liverpool now formally acknowledges its role in the slave trade, and in 1999 the City Council passed a formal motion unreservedly apologising for it. In 2007 Liverpool opened the International Slavery Museum as part of the Maritime Museum, with the aim of not only increasing understanding about the history of the trade but also campaigning on contemporary human rights issues.

4 Rise of the guild: competition for the MMSA

Whilst the MMSA finally, in 1880, chalked up a long-awaited success – Parliamentary agreement to grant the right of appeal against the findings of official Board of Trade inquiries, as well as changes to the composition of the tribunals – it began to face an increasing struggle to retain its members.

Early in 1893 a breakaway group – unhappy about the MMSA's closeness with shipowners, its apparent reluctance to push for increased pay and improved conditions, its 'close borough' governance, and its decision to allow marine superintendents to become members – established the Merchant Service Guild (MSG) under the leadership of John Grant Moore. Even though the guild's membership was restricted to certificated masters and officers of British nationality, within the space of five years it recruited more than 4,000 members – and only a decade after its launch, with more than 10,000 on its books, it was claiming to be the world's largest organisation for shipmasters and officers. Its rapid growth clearly rattled other bodies; in 1896 the London Society of Shipmasters was warned at its annual meeting that it was 'likely to be struck by a heavy blow' by the success of the guild.

The guild's prime objective was to 'unite into one body the certificated Captains and Officers of the British Empire, to enable them to demand and obtain a direct voice in the making of the laws and regulations by which they are governed'. Like the MMSA, it sought to influence government policy and provide professional and legal support to its members, while also striving to 'improve the position and status of the profession generally'. In its first year of existence the guild put forward proposals for improving the examinations for masters and officers, urged MPs to introduce the right of proxy voting for members away at sea, and wrote to British shipowners to call for three-watch working patterns, arguing that the four-on/four-off two-watch system 'brings about mental and physical strain which incapacitates the officers from properly attending their onerous and responsible duties whilst on watch and in charge of the ship'. It went on to submit a petition to the Board of Trade in January 1895, signed by more than 300 masters and officers, requesting improvements to the proposed 'rules of the road' for shipping.

The MSG had from the outset been very keen to emphasise its member-focused ways of organising itself, and its constitution was described by the *Journal of Commerce* as showing 'socialistic principles'. Whilst not describing itself as a trade union, the guild was perceived to be one by some of its members – including the Marquess of Graham (the elder son of the powerful Duke of Montrose), who was serving as navigating officer on board Lord Brassey's yacht *Sunbeam* and wrote of his membership: '*L'union fait la force*'. The guild used the same phrase – 'union is strength' – in December 1901, when it called for masters and officers to be more forthright in exposing unfair treatment and poor conditions of service. However, following an animated debate at the guild's 1907 annual meeting, its members rejected a proposal for it to be incorporated or to be registered as a friendly society, and in 1921 they voted by a substantial majority against the conversion of the guild into a trade union.

From its launch at a time when, as one contemporary magazine (*Scribner's*) wrote of ships' officers that 'in no other trade or profession is equal ability so badly paid', the guild was noticeably louder than the MMSA in speaking of the need for masters and officers to have decent pay and conditions. It became increasingly active in progressing demands for improved wages and paid leave entitlements on behalf of its members. At a time when there was no formal negotiating machinery, it did most of this by submitting petitions to company managements. In 1902, for example, it presented a petition to the Clan Line, signed by 161 of the company's officers, successfully protesting against the withdrawal of a daily 'safety money' allowance, and securing improved permanent pay rates amounting to increases of as much as £2 10s[6] to £3 per month. It also challenged the shipowner Walter Runciman over his claims about shipmasters' wages, pointing to the 'sadly precarious existence' of the members employed on a voyage-by-voyage basis. In the following year it supported members serving with Shell Transport and Trading who had refused to sail home from Singapore on the tanker *Telena* because they had been denied a dangerous cargo bonus for carrying benzene. It also challenged the Liverpool-based Larrinaga Line after it had reduced its certificated officer numbers, and switched from a three-watch to a two-watch system.

In 1913 the guild was involved in an early form of recognition dispute when a number of its members serving with P&O threatened to resign unless their

---

6 Currency until 1971 in the UK: £1 = 20s (shillings), and 1s = 12d (pence).

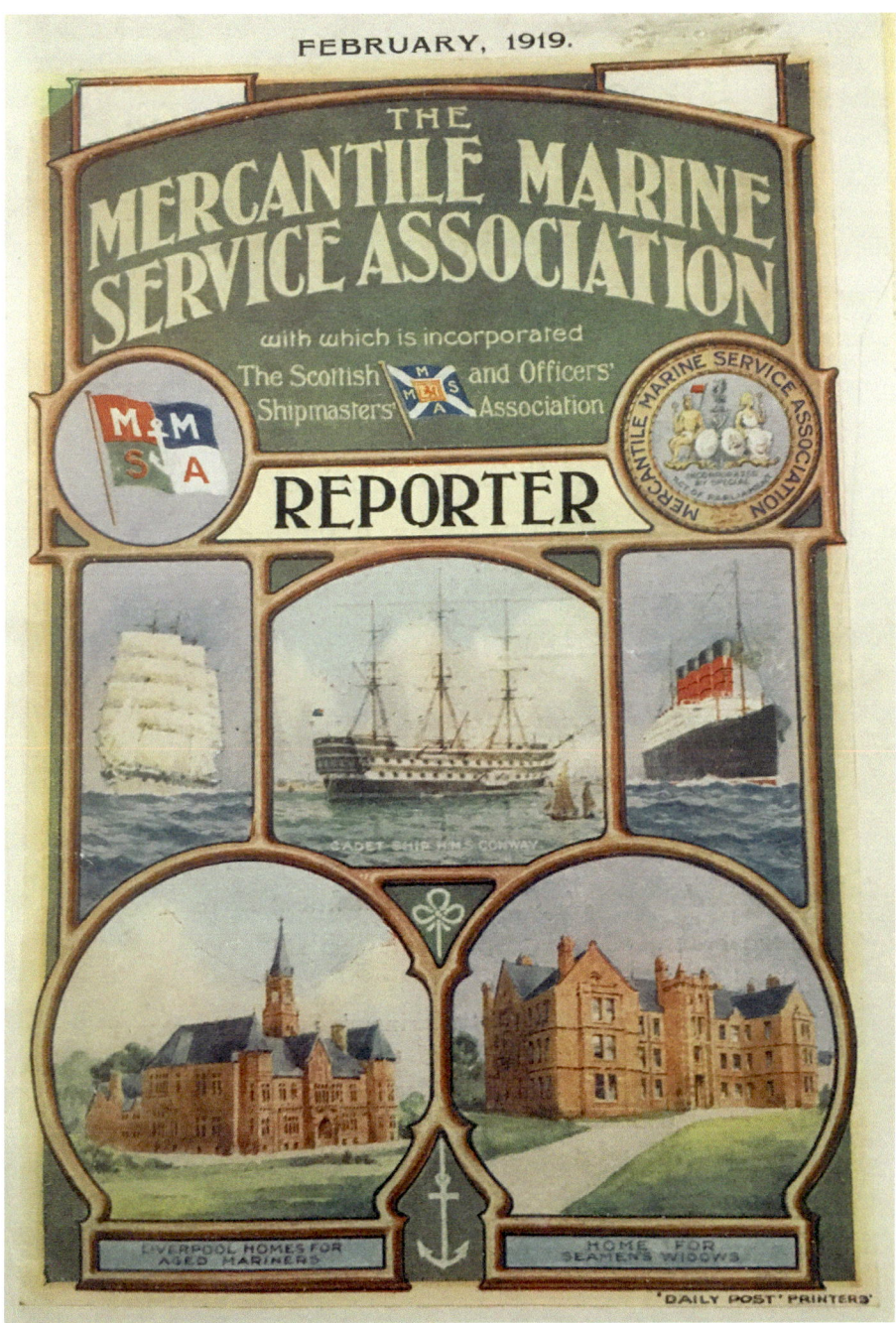

The MMSA's key functions were celebrated on the cover of its magazine in 1919 – but it was now facing strong competition from the rival Merchant Service Guild.

affairs were 'dealt with according to the views of the Merchant Service Guild'. In response, the P&O directors said it would be impossible 'to entertain the idea of allowing outsiders to dictate to the company in matters of this kind'. However, the company's continued refusal to address the officers' grievances – including pay, provision for old age, and an adequate holiday after long voyages – resulted in moves to stop ships sailing in October of that year. In a statement issued by the guild, Captain Moore complained:

> In the first place, the pay is wholly inadequate considering the multifarious duties and great responsibilities devolving upon the officers, in what is regarded the leading steamship company in the British mercantile marine. It is an extraordinary anomaly that in such a company, which has enjoyed long and unexampled prosperity, the pay is infinitely worse than in any of the other large lines.

In July of the following year IMSG members serving on MacBrayne steamers moved to take strike action after failing to receive a satisfactory response to their calls for 'substantial improvements' in remuneration and other conditions.

The guild campaigned on many of the same issues that exercised the MMSA, most notably on the criminalisation of members and the unrepresentative composition of many boards of inquiry. In 1898 it protested against the 'outrage' in which seven members of the crew of the steamship *Greylands* had been detained in a Buenos Aires prison for five months without trial or inquiry. In the following year it successfully lobbied against 'a gross miscarriage of justice' in which, following a collision off the coast of Malta, a chief officer member, Edward Kemp, not only had his certificate suspended for six months but also was arrested on a charge of manslaughter.

Like the MMSA, the guild was a strong advocate for professional standards, taking early action to lobby the Board of Trade over the dangers of allowing coastal vessels to be operated by uncertificated captains and officers, as well organising a long-running campaign for the introduction of light loadline regulations to ensure that ships went to sea with sufficient ballast. It mounted a spirited attack on shipowners' 'extraordinary' proposals to allow apprentices to obtain a third mate's certificate after three years' service, and a fourth mate's after two, with no examinations 'and without the slightest guarantee as to their proficiency'. It also managed to secure a Parliamentary debate on proposals to outlaw the carriage of deck loads in the North Atlantic in winter months, and made repeated representations over the 'woefully bad condition' of the life-saving equipment on many vessels. In one of the rare examples of inter-organisational cooperation at this time, in April 1913 the guild joined with the MMSA and the Marine Engineers' Association (MEA) to form a deputation to the Board of Trade, calling for an international agreement to ban the carriage of heavy loads on decks.

The guild's Parliamentary lobbying also included pressure for an official inquiry into issues including the responsibilities and remuneration of British masters and officers, 'the rest and recreation afforded to them; the necessity of British ships being manned with a sufficient number of British certified officers; [and] increasing the standard of the present Board of Trade examinations'. However, when the government finally agreed to such an inquiry, the guild refused to take part in the ensuing deliberations because it considered the composition of the committee to be unrepresentative.

The guild also spared no effort in standing up for the maritime profession – for example, writing to the *British Medical Journal* in 1910 to complain about a doctor describing seafarers as heavy drinkers. General Secretary Thomas Moore (the son of Captain John Moore, the founder of the guild) pointed out that with typical daily working days of 15 to 16 hours, many masters and officers simply had no free time to drink, and that in the previous year 'out of approximately some 30,000 certificated Captains and officers of the merchant service, not a dozen had their certificates suspended on the score of alcoholic excess'.

When in 1907 British shipowners said they wanted to attract a 'better class' of young men to the merchant service, the guild angrily defended its members: 'We are proud to say that despite the manifest difficulties under which they labour and the discouraging treatment they frequently receive, members of the cloth as a whole not only consider themselves, but are, Officers and gentlemen.'

However, both the guild and the MMSA had noted the changing status of shipmasters; the growing scope of maritime regulation was increasing their accountability and their exposure to legal action at the very time when the shipping companies were increasingly treating their commanders as just another disposable employee. 'Time was when the Master of a British merchant ship was monarch of all he surveyed,' the *Guild Gazette* ruefully reflected in August 1907. 'The formation of shipping companies with neither soul nor sentiment led up to those who ran their ships being looked upon as mere automata in the game.'

Throughout its history, the MMSA was strong in its advocacy of the need for firm onboard discipline, and in 1904 the evidence it presented to the Mercantile Marine Committee meant that its call for the Board of Trade to introduce a power to punish crew members for 'insolent or contemptuous language or behaviour to the master or officers' was successful.

Seamen's union leader Havelock Wilson, seated second left and sporting a fine moustache, spoke at the 26th annual meeting of the Merchant Service Guild, where he warned: 'It is no good for us to talk in this country about compelling our shipowners to pay larger wages, give better food, accommodation and safety regulations if we allow in our ports in this country, or the empire, alien ships to come in where they are able to work at 25% and 30% less cost than ours.'

During this period the guild became increasingly active in seeking to get a clear legal distinction between the roles and responsibilities of shipmasters and pilots – noting that 'whatever happens, it seems that the Captain goes to the wall'. It also argued strongly for masters to be defined as 'seamen' for the purposes of entitlement to the provisions of the Workmen's Compensation Act.

Measures to reduce long working hours were an early target for the guild, which highlighted the way in which masters and officers were 'expected to work uncomplainingly for twelve, fourteen, sixteen or even twenty hours in the day without the slightest recompense being offered to them'. Noting the resulting threats to safety, it argued for the adoption of the three-watch system as a more sensible way of running a vessel. In particular, by deploying medical advice on the adverse effects of excessive hours it succeeding in persuading Cunard Line to operate special watchkeeping rotas that sought to minimise fatigue. In 1920 the guild worked with the National Sailors' and Firemen's Union (NSFU) to jointly lobby for the introduction of an eight-hour day for all seafarers in the merchant service.

Among the guild's early campaign successes was the introduction in 1900 of a compulsory continuous discharge system for British seamen, with the government accepting its core argument that this would help to improve discipline on board by enabling the ability and conduct (and sobriety) of individuals to be formally recorded. The guild also fought hard for the adoption of the Mariners' Votes Bill, to enable seafarers to record a vote when they would be at sea, and it won a battle for 'distressed' masters and officers to be repatriated in 'proper' conditions, scuppering shipowners' attempts to make them pay their own passage home after a shipwreck.

In response to inquiries from members about income tax liabilities, the guild secured in 1901 what it described as an 'important' response from the Inland Revenue, confirming that master mariners were entitled to exemptions if 'absent from the United Kingdom' for six months or more in any tax year, and it went on to assist members in winning back as much as three years' worth of overpayments. However, in 1904 the Revenue, appearing to make a U-turn, told the guild that it had been 'legally advised that all mariners signing articles and being paid off in the United Kingdom are liable for the tax'. This policy was reversed in September 1917, when the guild was informed that officers on merchant ships would be entitled to the same reduced rates of income tax as those serving in the Royal Navy and the Army.

The guild made repeated efforts to tackle what it regarded as the unfair competition faced by the British shipping industry, calling for coastal trades to be reserved for British-flagged ships, and floating the idea of a nationalised merchant fleet. In November 1912 its lobbying secured a lengthy House of Lords debate on the need for 'urgent and effective attention' to be given 'to grievances affecting the commanders and officers of the mercantile marine in respect to insufficiency of pay, inferior accommodation, undue hours of labour, and other matters which are of serious moment to the mercantile marine as a whole'.

In its quest to improve onboard conditions, the guild made repeated protests about the 'utterly inadequate' standards for seafarers' accommodation, pointing out that a seaman was entitled to just 72 cu ft of space on a ship, as opposed to a requirement for 300 cu ft per head in common lodging houses, 600 cu ft per head in Army barracks – and 800 cu ft per cow in cowsheds. It also pressed the Board of Trade for nautical cookery schools to be established in major ports, and called for certification for ships' cooks to 'remedy the crying evil of bad cooking and spoiled food onboard ships'.

With the use of red and green navigation lights becoming increasingly common in the middle of the 19th century, the British government decided in 1877 to introduce colour vision tests for candidates for mates and masters' certificates. Both the MSG and the MMSA raised growing concerns over the adequacy and fairness of the tests, and in 1914 the guild presented a petition to Parliament signed by more than 10,000 masters and officers calling for the Board of Trade to introduce an improved system for assessments. This led to the adoption of the lantern tests, which were successfully used for the next 100-plus years.

However, during that period the bitter rivalry between the MSG and the MMSA was so intense that, as Alan Villiers wrote in *The Navigators and the Merchant Navy*, it 'mitigated against any effective results from their representations to shipowners', and officers 'became either despondent, angry, or philosophically accepted the fact that apparently nothing could ever be done effectively to remedy their undoubted grievances'. From the outset the guild had been scathing in its criticism of the MMSA, accusing it of being unrepresentative, failing to provide an effective voice for maritime professionals and not protecting captains and officers from 'villainous attacks and gratuitous insults'.

There was a very public dispute between the guild and the Shipmasters' and Officers' Federation (consisting of the MMSA, the British Shipmasters' Protection Society of Sunderland, the London-based Shipmasters' Society and the Scottish Shipmasters' Association) over the scale of their respective roles in bringing the Flag Bill before Parliament in an attempt to secure regulations to limit the command of British ships to British subjects. The guild had taken an assertive position against what it regarded as the growing threat to British jobs, arguing that the abolition of such rules through the repeal of the Navigation Act in 1849 had been 'ill-advised', and pointing out that in 1896 there had been 748 foreign masters and mates working on UK-registered vessels.

The MMSA had similarly highlighted its concerns about the growing use of non-national seafarers. At its 1900 AGM it told its members that the percentage of foreign crews on British ships had risen from 7 per cent in 1858 to 27 per cent in 1898. In the same period, it warned, the number of apprentices on British ships had declined from 5,578 to 2,359.

The guild's tireless Parliamentary representative, Lord Muskerry, supported successive attempts – fiercely opposed by the owners – to introduce legislation to restrict the issue of Board of Trade certificates of competency to British masters and mates of any grade, and to prevent foreign nationals from serving as marine pilots in British waters.

In contrast to its frosty relations with the MMSA, the guild made a formal alliance with the Marine Engineers' Association in 1913, both organisations emphasising the common interests of the masters and the deck and engineer officers, and warning that 'the Shipping Federation would have to reckon with a powerful combination'.

From its early days, the guild also built strong international connections – most notably in India, China, Canada and New Zealand. In an early example of the cross-border cooperation pursued by its successors, the guild established a reciprocal agreement with the Mercantile Marine Officers' Association in Shanghai, providing mutual temporary membership and support to visiting members. In 1904 these connections led to the proposal to add 'Imperial' to the guild's title, and in 1906 members attending the AGM agreed to a proposal to amend the title along these lines. Putting the suggestion forward, the guild's general secretary, Thomas Moore, noted that 'there are several other Guilds existing now and it is necessary to take that step in advance in case they adopt that title'.

In 1916 the guild claimed to have more than 16,000 members on its books. and two years later it merged with the Sunderland-based British Shipmasters' and Officers' Protection Society, which had been established in 1873 with the core aim of providing legal support to those involved in marine inquiries, and in 1899 had helped to form the Certificated Officers' Union. But, perhaps unsurprisingly, the guild failed to build on its early successes, and after the First World War and the death of Captain John Moore its membership began to decline, dropping to less than 5,000 by the early 1920s. One reason for this was the creation of a new organisation, the British Merchant Service League (BMSL), in 1919. Formed by a group of Merchant Navy officers who had served with the Royal Naval Reserve during the war and registered as a trade union in April 1920, the league sought to 'unite the two great branches of the service – the navigating and the engineering officers – into one great union for the promotion and protection of their professional interests'. Its leaders argued that unity was vital at a time of growing officer unemployment and cuts in their pay, and they unsuccessfully invited the IMSG, the MMSA and the MEA to join forces as a single union outside the umbrella of the National Maritime Board to resist the owners' plans to slash officers' wages by £4 10s a month (more about this in Chapter 7).

The BMSL set itself a series of ambitious aims, including increased pay, allowances for uniforms, subsistence money in port, 21 days of annual leave, a 56-hour working week at sea and a 44-hour week in port. It chalked up a successful action early in 1921, when it organised a lightning strike on board the Canadian Pacific liner *Corsica* to reverse cuts in officer numbers. Although the action had been supported by members of the NSFU, the league was opposed to the concept of officer unions working alongside ratings' representatives, arguing that this had the effect of depressing officers' pay and conditions, and it sought to operate outside the Seafarers' Joint Council. The union grew rapidly and by August that year was claiming to have recruited 9,427 members. But by the end of the year it had crashed and burned, blaming its failure to prosper on the slump in the shipping industry, which had curtailed its ability to organise strikes to oppose shipowners' plans to cut officers' pay.

Interestingly, when ratings union leader Havelock Wilson addressed the IMSG annual meeting in 1919 he told how he had only recently spoken at a meeting in Portsmouth with those seeking to organise the new officers' union. 'First of all, they had got the idea that a union sounded better than a Guild,' he said. 'But to my mind, I do not care what you call it. It is not the question of the name of an organisation: it is the question of whether it will perform all that it promises.'

However, the league was not the first attempt to create a fully fledged trade union for officers. In May 1912 the National Union of Masters and Mates (NUMM) had been established, having as 'its object the improvement of salaries paid and the conditions of service obtaining in the greater number of the shipping companies'.

The NUMM attracted some attention after it appointed a baronet, Sir Charles Louis, as its treasurer. Explaining his decision to take up the post, Sir Charles – who had spent 35 years working at sea – said: 'My lengthy experience of the mercantile marine has convinced me of the great need for reform in wages and conditions in the service.' The NUMM offered the post of president to Father Charles Hopkins, who had played an important role in the UK seamen's strike of 1911 and had also organised a union for seafarers while he was working in India.

The NUMM had a brief flurry of activity, seeking to organise a series of national strikes by officers in August 1912 to advance its claim for a scale of wages linked to the gross tonnage of ships, and for an overtime rate of one shilling an hour. It managed to stop a couple of Canadian Pacific ships, *Mount Royal* and *Montreal*, in the port of London, and Fr Hopkins was called in to mediate after a chief officer member was dismissed by the company for refusing to do dockers' work.

Some reports suggested that the IMSG had organised the stoppages, but General Secretary Thomas Moore wrote to *The Scotsman* to dissociate itself from the action. However, he also noted the 'immense amount of dissatisfaction' that existed among officers – especially those in the coastal trades – and warned that 'the time has arrived when radical changes and improvements' in their conditions were required.

The NUMM appealed to the IMSG to support the strike plans, arguing that a significant number of guild members were in favour of 'more militant action', and pointing out that one of the six companies facing the action had agreed to increase its officers' pay by £1 a month. However, there appeared to be little appetite for the dispute, and the Canadian Pacific ships sailed with new crew brought in to replace the strikers. Although the NUMM warned that there could be 'another battle royal of the lines of the great sea strike of 1911' if pay talks failed to deliver in the following year, its threat of an 'alliance with the sailors and firemen' or a 'simultaneous attack upon the shipowners' failed to materialise. The union's membership struggled to top more than a couple of hundred during its existence and, perhaps unsurprisingly, it was dissolved in 1914.

Somewhat more significant impact had been generated by the National Certificated Shipmasters' and Officers' Union of Great Britain and Ireland (subsequently renamed the Union of Shipmasters and Officers, and frequently referred to as the Shipmasters' and Officers' Union: SOU). Established in South Shields early in 1889, it merged in July of the following year with its bitter rival, the Sunderland-based National Amalgamated Certificated Officers' Union, which had sought to elevate the professional, moral, financial and political status of its members, 'to bring back that confidence between them and their employers which had been destroyed through the keen competition of the profession … and to remedy the many grievances which it laboured under'.

At its peak the SOU was reported to have had more than 20 branches nationwide and as many as 9,000 members, with the great campaigner Samuel Plimsoll accepting an invitation to become an honorary member. In September 1890 it was part of a 40-strong seafarers' delegation to the Trades Union Congress in Liverpool, and it adopted a strong set of objectives including increased wages, mutual assistance in gaining employment, death and sickness benefits, certificate protection, and support for 'all legal claims and defences incidental to a member's calling', with leaders noting how officers' wages had fallen behind the pay of engineers and many ratings. One master mariner member summed things up in a letter to the *Shields Gazette*:

> The masters complain that the chief engineer is better paid by £2 per month than them. In some cases the first mate from £2 10s to £3 less than the second engineer. What is the reason? One single word: Combination. Nine out of ten masters and mates are heart and soul with the Union, but are afraid to join of their own free will for fear of losing employment.

The union analysed the wages paid to its members working from ten of the country's biggest ports, and developed detailed proposals for 'fair minimum rates for each trade and size of ship and steamer'; these were submitted to the shipowners in October 1890.

From the outset the new officers' union had a close working relationship with the rapidly expanding National Amalgamated Sailors and Firemen's Union (ultimately to become the National Union of Seamen). NASFU general secretary Havelock Wilson served as manager of the SOU until December 1890, when Captain George Lucock was appointed general secretary and Captain J.W. Wright became the new manager. The union stated optimistically: 'The shipowners having put forward Mr Wilson's connection with the society as an objection, it is now hoped that this objection no longer exists [and] friendly negotiations will be opened up for the revision of the scale.'

In the previous month Havelock Wilson had addressed a special meeting of the SOU, telling members that the time had now arrived when he intended to organise them into a firm body and that he would base the union 'upon a rock that would require an earthquake to shake it'. Shipmasters and deck officers were now, he added, 'about the only class of men who were not organised and protected by trades unionism and could safely be called the most persecuted race of men of this island'.

At the end of November the NASFU sent an instruction to its seafaring and firefighting members, telling them not to sign articles on ships whose master and officers were not members of the officers' union.

In the following month, the union's South Shields branch heard that the Coal Heavers' Union in the port of London had given a significant gesture of solidarity, stating its determination that each master and officer of coasting steamers trading to London should produce their membership card before coal cargoes could be discharged.

In September 1890 shipowners – alarmed by the looming prospect of the industrial muscle flowing from unity between officers and ratings – had responded by setting up the Shipping Federation as 'a fighting machine to counter the strike weapon'. The link between the officers' and ratings' unions was, Havelock Wilson recalled, 'the last straw in encouraging the shipowners to establish their powerful organisation'.

The federation's executive council moved rapidly, sending a circular to its members stating that

> it is of the utmost importance that all shipowners should at once warn their masters, officers and engineers against being coerced into joining the so-called 'Union of Shipmasters and Officers of Great Britain and Ireland', or any other union or society not under the control of its own members. It is hardly necessary to point out that such demands on the part of the crew, if acceded to by shipowners, must at once deprive the masters and officers of that self-respect and independence without which discipline cannot be maintained, and vessels so commanded must eventually become risks that neither ship nor cargo underwriters can willingly cover at usual rates.

By the end of 1890 the federation boasted a membership of owners representing more than 85 per cent of total UK tonnage. It had opened offices in all the main ports, and insisted upon seafarers being engaged through those offices, with the use of a 'ticket' that gave the holder preference in securing work on ships owned by federation members. It also worked closely with the newly formed Federated Association of Shipmasters and Officers (which comprised the MMSA, the British Shipmasters' and Officers' Protection Society of Sunderland, the London-based Shipmasters' Society and the Scottish Shipmasters' Association) whose founding principles included protecting 'members against the coercion which is being practised to force them to join certain trades unions'. The fact that in September 1890 these organisations had sent a deputation to the federation makes it clear that they were not only alarmed by the potential for shipboard discipline to be undermined by a single union but were also expecting their loyalty to the owners to be rewarded, as they went on to submit detailed proposals for improvements in pay and changes to watchkeeping systems.

Within the space of three years more than 100,000 ratings, 5,800 masters and officers, and 1,400 engineers had 'taken the Federation ticket'. The Shipping Federation's effective use of divide and rule tactics, coupled with blackleg labour to undermine industrial action and a concerted flurry of lawsuits, saw off the officers' union, and the NASFU membership tumbled from 78,000 in 1891 to just 5,000 three years later, at which point the union went into voluntary liquidation. This, however, was by no means its death knell, nor did it make the Shipping Federation redundant.

5 Oil and water: the early engineers' union

In the early 1800s steam had started to transform the shipping industry and with it the profile of the seafaring workforce. In 1820 just 34 foreign-going steamers were registered in the UK fleet; a decade later the figure had risen to 298, and by 1841 it stood at 793. Between 1860 and 1900 the proportion of the fleet that was steam-powered rose from just over 30 per cent to more than 90 per cent.

The first wave of seagoing engineers had no ship-specific qualifications or formal training, and were usually employed on the basis of recommendations from shore-based engineering firms and dockyards. However, as steam engine technology developed and the roles and responsibilities of the marine engineer rose, there were increasing calls for the introduction of government regulations in line with the requirements for navigating officers. Whilst the early marine engineers were relatively well paid, a first engineer having a higher salary than a mate, they faced a struggle to get full recognition of their importance, despite the introduction of engineers' Certificates of Competence through the 1862 Merchant Shipping Acts Amendment Act. Shipowners, apparently resenting the extra costs of engineers, made repeated efforts to keep their numbers as low as possible.

Fed up with such pressures, engineers began to organise themselves. In 1877 the Liverpool Association of Marine Engineers was established following an inaugural meeting at The Temple. But although it had the objectives of giving members 'opportunities for self-improvement, tending towards elevating them in the social position', it never seemed to gain more than 500 members and disappeared a few years later. In 1879, in a similar spirit of self-help, the United Kingdom Association of Sea-going Engineers began to set up branches in ports such as Cardiff, Sunderland and Shields. It had the aim of opening lodges in all the UK's major ports, but it too faded away after a couple of years.

Discontent, however, did not disappear, and on 8 February 1887 a group of engineer officers met in London to discuss their concerns over cuts in pay and reductions in engine-room crewing. They agreed that a union was needed to protect their interests, and backed a proposal to sound out colleagues about the creation of such an organisation.

Within the space of just one month 200 potential members were gathered during visits to vessels in the docks, and a second meeting, held in one of the committee rooms at Limehouse Town Hall in London, unanimously agreed to the formation of a Marine Engineers' Union (MEU) 'which shall be devoted entirely to their interests, managed exclusively by themselves, and have for its objects the assertion and maintenance of their rights, redress for their wrong, and improvement in their remuneration and treatment'.

The first member's card was issued on 18 March 1877, and by the end of the year the union had a membership of more than 1,200, with branches formed in London, Liverpool, Cardiff, Newport, Glasgow, Sunderland, South Shields, Hartlepool, Antwerp and Hamburg.

The MEU's early success in securing pay rises and protecting engine-room crewing levels helped to generate significant growth, with membership rising to more than 8,000 by the end of 1890. As well as tackling working conditions, the union lobbied MPs for reforms in training and certification requirements, as well as presenting proposals for a portion of wages to be advanced to members' families each week to ease the financial pressures on them during their breadwinners' long absences. In 1891 general secretary William Marshall made a call to the Royal Commission on Labour for the introduction of a standard international wage for seafarers irrespective of where they lived.

From the outset, the MEU had recognised the importance of collective organisation and was not afraid to take industrial action. It staged a successful stoppage of its Hull-based members in 1897 to secure an improved pay offer for the coastal and home trades; in the following year its members serving with Glasgow-based Allan Line held a strike, seeking to secure increased pay and overtime allowances, but it was unsuccessful.

The union also worked hard to raise the professional status of marine engineers, staging lectures on subjects of technical interest at its branches. In 1901 the general secretary proudly told a meeting in South Shields that the union's branches were serving as educational institutions, and it had floated the idea of creating a college for marine engineers.

The union fought hard to resist the 'insidious' imposition of the Shipping Federation's 'ticket' on its members, complaining against the 'tyranny' under which chief engineers could no longer select their own firemen. It also represented some members who had been dismissed for refusing to register with the shipowners and protested against the federation's attempts to reduce pay rates.

Only seven years after the MEU had been formed it achieved one of its core objectives, with the 1894 Merchant Shipping Act formally recognising seagoing engineers as officers. In the same year – and partly in response to the MEU's representations – the Board of Trade agreed to establish a Committee on Undermanning in the Mercantile Marine. However, the resulting non-mandatory recommendations failed to set any scale for engine-room personnel, even though there was compelling evidence to show that there had been some fairly savage cuts in crewing levels over the previous 20 years. In 1897 the MEU went on to work with the MMSA, the London-based Shipmasters' Society and the UK Pilots' Association, in order to promote the adoption by Parliament of the Certificated Officers' Bill. The proposed regulations would have stipulated the carriage of certificated officers on British ships, along with stipulations on the numbers to be carried, together with a requirement that no certificates for masters, mates, engineers or pilots should be issued by the UK to anyone other than a British subject. Although the move was unsuccessful in 1897, the battle for tighter controls was to continue for many more years, culminating in a wartime ruling in 1916 that 'no aliens, whether nationalised or not, are to be in command of British steamers'.

The MEU also made another significant achievement in securing Board of Trade agreement to appoint engineers to local marine boards around the UK, and it followed this up with a successful campaign to have engineer assessors at courts of inquiry into shipping casualties whenever the interests of engineers were at stake.

From its early years the MEU operated an employment bureau to find jobs for its members, and it also established a non-contributory accidental death bonus scheme in 1897 in response to statistics showing the high loss of life amongst seagoing engineers.

In 1899 the MEU renamed itself the Marine Engineers' Association, on the grounds that the new title 'was more in keeping with the development of the professional status of the membership'. The decision reflected sentiments that had been summed up in a member's letter to the union's journal a few years before:

> Dear Sir – Is it not time that we leave the rank of unionist and advance to something better? Outsiders class us with 'Sailors and Firemen', 'Coalheavers', 'Dock Labourers', 'Cooks and Stewards' and other kindred unionists, and look upon us as occupying a position socially inferior … we, as men of average intelligence, education and experience, deserve a combination on a higher level than unionists.

However, the name change did nothing to dilute the strength of the organisation's campaigning, and it waged what it described as 'unceasing war' against the shipowners over their attempts to exclude seafarers from the Workmen's Compensation Acts. In 1904 the MEA sent a deputation to the home secretary, and in July 1907 it lobbied MPs to ensure that the legislation was extended to seafarers.

The MEA echoed the demands of other officers' organisations for improved onboard accommodation. In 1906 its Grand Council chairman, Sir Fortescue Flannery, stated that 'when the accommodation on board steamers was improved, and all the arrangements on board were such that engineers could be treated as officers and gentlemen as well as engineers, the best men could be attracted to those vessels'.

The MEA also continued to press for higher professional standards, successfully arguing for an extended period of apprenticeship to be brought in with effect from January 1904. It made the case for the introduction of a third-class certificate, and in May 1906 sent a deputation to the Board of Trade to support its calls for more stringent requirements on engineer numbers to reflect increases in tonnage, higher pressures and the greater speed of modern steamers.

From 1892 the union had been involved in an early formal collective negotiating body – the North-East Coast of England Marine Engineers' Conciliation Board – which covered the pay and conditions of around 1,300 engineer officers. However, in 1911 the MEA's general council decided that it was time to seek a standard set of rates, so it began what was to be a successful drive to harmonise a diverse range of local and sectional agreements for engineer officers, together with significant pay rises to reflect the increased responsibilities and the 'larger vessels, more complicated machinery and numerous auxiliary machineries' that its members were having to deal with. To support the claim, the MEA obtained details of improvements in pay and conditions that had recently been secured by the Danish Marine Engineers' Union, and it also argued for measures to reduce the working hours of engineer officers, especially work in excess of time on watch.

Grievances over pay were marked. In 1911 members serving on Lancashire & Yorkshire Railway Company steamers staged a successful stoppage for higher pay, and in 1913 a strike by MEA members serving on Nelson Line ships managed to secure increased wages and better hours after they stopped four of the company's ships from sailing. In October of the same year the Royal Mail Steamship Packet Company also agreed to improve wages following a stoppage organised by the MEA.

In the previous year, following talks with the Shipping Federation, the MEA had agreed to the establishment of the first national wage scale for engineer officers. It followed this up with action in June 1914 to support a claim for further improvements in the pay rates – with demands for an increase of 40 shillings a month for chief and second engineers, and 30 shillings a month for third and fourth engineers. Following a ballot of members early in the year, when talks with the Shipping Federation had broken down, the MEA issued instructions to its members to refuse to sign articles on board tramp ships unless the increases were paid and the owners agreed to discuss overtime, excessive work hours and leave. The action was effective, stopping ships in many major ports, and as more and more owners offered the higher rates those who tried to hold out against the claim often found their vessels unable to sail as a result of insufficient engineer officers. Within a month of the dispute the MEA reported that while the increases had been granted to members serving on around 300 ships, the action would continue until there was a national agreement. The dispute raised national concerns about the movement of South Wales coal and its knock-on effect upon industry, and a sign of its significance came when the First Lord of the Admiralty was brought in to 'bring about a speedy and successful termination of the strike'. The Shipping Federation finally agreed to set up a committee to deal with the claim in June, but refused once more to make any increases – citing 'the present state of trade and foreign competition'. Soon after war broke out in August, the MEA agreed to call off the dispute, subject to all engineer officers unemployed as a result of the dispute being reinstated to their positions.

Like the other officers' organisations, the MEA had a strong focus on safety, and this was brought into sharp focus when 25 of the union's members lost their lives in the *Titanic* disaster. The MEA made a successful application for representation at the inquiry along with the Imperial Merchant Service Guild. It is somewhat sad to note that six years before the *Titanic*'s loss the MEA had called for owners to install alarms in engine rooms to indicate when all hope of saving a ship had been lost.

The Southampton memorial to the 35 engineer officers who died in the Titanic *disaster. Six years before the loss the MEA had been pressing for alarms to enable the prompt evacuation of engine rooms.*

The MEA also played a prominent role in the long-running and ultimately successful battle to ensure that seafarers could vote while away from home, with the 1918 Representation of the People Act giving them the right to vote by proxy in Parliamentary elections.

The MEA had from 1910 taken an active part in the increasingly intense battle to persuade shipowners to establish a General Superannuation Scheme for Officers of the Mercantile Marine, to 'remove the gaunt spectre of poverty in old age which has haunted the sea-going life of many an officer in the past'. While some of the larger companies introduced pension schemes of their own around this time, the majority remained opposed to the introduction of a general scheme for some years to come.

The MEA had also been part of another early quest for collaboration, joining with other officers' organisations in 1906 to make a united call to the Board of Trade for officers and seamen to be given the right to 'call in an official of the Society to which they belonged' in the event of a dispute at paying-off time. Despite strong shipowner opposition, the Board of Trade said it recognised the justice of allowing 'a properly accredited person' to represent officers in such situations, and that it had given the necessary instructions to the superintendents of Mercantile Marine offices.

In a further step towards a greater sense of common purpose, the MEA and the IMSG announced in December 1913 that they had agreed to embark on a 'policy of cooperation', and to work jointly on such issues as safety at sea and members' wages. Announcing their 'friendly understanding', the two organisations stated that they recognised the importance of collaborating in such areas, noting that their common approach could provide 'a still more powerful lever'. Just four years later, they were to be among the founder members of what was to be described as 'a new era' of industrial relations in shipping.

6 Sparks fly: rise of the Radio Officers' Union

Steam power was not the only technology reshaping shipping and seafaring at the close of the 19th century. In 1900 the German liner *Kaiser Wilhelm der Gross* became the first ship to be fitted with Marconi's wireless telegraphy system, sending the first ship-to-shore wireless message in March that year. In 1901 the Elder Dempster vessel *Lake Champlain* became the first British ship to carry wireless equipment, and by June 1913 some 686 ships on transatlantic services were using Marconi's wireless stations.

Many owners were initially reluctant to invest in the cost of the equipment, and before the First World War most of the vessels fitted with wireless were large passenger ships. But because cargo operators were becoming increasingly aware that they could actually save money or prevent losses by using the technology to route their ships away from danger or summon assistance if they were in trouble, the use of wireless started to spread to large cargo-carrying vessels.

The vital safety role of marine wireless was underlined in the loss of the passenger ships *Titanic* in 1912 and *Empress of Ireland* in 1914, and wireless had also attracted wide public attention when it was used to catch the murderer Dr Hawley Harvey Crippen on board *Montrose* in 1910. The *Titanic* disaster resulted in an international conference on safety at sea, held in London in 1913 and attended by delegates from 65 countries. Its recommendations included having a 24-hour wireless watch on all ships. The UK followed on from this with the 1914 Merchant Shipping Convention Bill, which sought compulsory carriage of wireless equipment by all ships carrying more than 50 passengers. Although the Bill was passed by the House of Commons, the outbreak of war meant that it was not enacted; however, in 1916 the Defence of the Realm Act was approved, requiring all ships of 1,600 grt and above to be fitted with wireless.

The number of marine wireless operators consequently soared, with 'urgent demand' for their services leading the government to exempt young men studying for the qualifications from military service. By the end of the war, the number of wireless operators had trebled, to more than 4,500, to enable continuous watches to be kept on each ship, and in 1919 the government introduced the Merchant Shipping (Wireless Telegraphy) Bill to require every passenger steamer or every cargo vessel of 1,600 grt and above to have a wireless telegraphy installation, and 'operators and watchers as may be necessary'.

Until the war the Marconi company had had a virtual monopoly on the training and supply of wireless operators, and it had actively opposed employees' repeated attempts to set up a representative body. However, in 1912 the Postal Telegraph Clerks' Association was asked to help establish the Association of Wireless Telegraphists (AWT), which was successfully achieved by the end of the year, with an inaugural membership of 55. The organisation's growth was pretty spectacular, rising from 279 members in 1913 to 1,576 in 1917 and some 4,500 by the end of the war. Initially headquartered in Liverpool, the AWT was quick to set out its core aims: raising the pay and conditions of its members. General Secretary E.R. Tuck complained that wireless operators, 'hailed as a hero at times of disaster', were paid less than anyone else on a ship – 'even lower than trimmers and firemen'. Calling for recognition by the Marconi company, the AWT warned that without a significant increase in pay, the work of its members would be 'nothing more than a blind alley occupation'.

With an impressive membership density of more than 90 per cent, the AWT soon managed to overcome owners' opposition to its membership of the National Maritime Board Seafarers' Joint Council, and in 1918 it was formally recognised as the representative body for wireless operators. It took an early lead in tackling the inherent challenges of organising a fragmented membership by establishing an 'honorary delegate' system to assist recruitment and to provide a two-way flow of information between the union and its seagoing members.

The AWT was markedly more militant than other officers' organisations, and in April 1919 its threat to take strike action secured a climbdown by Marconi over its failure to apply a backdated £3 a month war risk payment that had been agreed at the National Maritime Board (NMB). Then in 1920 the strength and commitment of the AWT and its members was sorely tested when strike action was organised following the failure to progress a claim filed in September 1919. This had called for the wage structure to be revised in order to bring the pay of wireless operators more into line with that of officers than – as it had been before the war – with that of ratings.

The ten-day stoppage was well supported by AWT members – and, significantly, secured the support of the MMSA, the IMSG, the MEA and the ratings' unions. The action proved highly effective, despite the government's attempts to undermine it by informing shipowners that the requirement to carry wireless operators would not be enforced; questioned in Parliament, the Board of Trade President Sir Robert Horne defended the move on the grounds that 'to hold up the shipping of this country with the effect of inflicting untold hardship on the whole community which is dependent upon overseas supplies would be unjustifiable'.

Nevertheless, after getting assurances from owners that there would be no sackings and that any settlement would be backdated, the AWT returned to the negotiating table in August 1920, and secured a significant increase in pay and increments for its members, more than doubling the rates that they had been on at the outbreak of the First World War.

The celebrations proved short-lived, however, as in March 1921 the shipowners proposed pay cuts for all seafarers in response to poor trading conditions. The AWT claimed that the cuts fell disproportionately on its members and took the matter to arbitration. In a judgment announced on 1 June 1921 the Industrial Court sided with the union's arguments about 'the position of responsibility and education required of a wireless telegraphist' and ruled in favour of a level of pay reductions lower than those of other groups of seafarers.

In the same year the AWT amalgamated with the Cable and Telegraph Operators' Association, to form the Association of Wireless and Cable Telegraphists (AWCT). The new union was put to the test when the employers put forward further proposals to slash pay by up to 20 per cent. Talks broke down after the companies not only refused to drop the plans but also sought to impose additional duties upon wireless operators. A 16-day strike followed, and the resulting negotiations ended with agreement on a 10 per cent pay cut.

The dispute also led to a significant decision, hailed as beneficial to all

The June 1921 issue of the AWT journal The Radiograph *contained a detailed account of an arbitration award which protected its members from the worst excesses of pay cuts being imposed upon British seafarers at the time.*

workers, when the AWCT secured a Ministry of Labour ruling that 'an applicant for unemployment benefit is not disentitled to the receipt of benefit by reason only that he has declined an offer of employment in a situation vacant in consequence of his stoppage of work due to a trade dispute'.

In November 1925 the AWCT once again called its members out on strike in response to yet more proposals for pay cuts. And once again, the Board of Trade gave the green light for companies to operate their ships without wireless operators. Questioned in Parliament, Board of Trade president Arthur Samuel defended the decision to waive safety rules on the ground that 'it is necessary that our sea trade should proceed so that poor people who receive their food from abroad should not be put to extra expense for extra cost of food owing to detention of ships'.

By January 1926 some 2,000 wireless operators were on strike, and nearly all of them had been dismissed by their companies. The AWCT demanded a court of inquiry into the dispute, but the Ministry of Labour instead set up fresh talks between the union and the employers. The strike was suspended on 19 February 1926, when the companies agreed to reinstate sacked AWCT members and have the case heard by the Industrial Court. The ensuing judgment resulted in a reduced level of pay cuts, and it aligned wireless operators' salaries with those of deck officers. But it also introduced what the union described as the 'iniquitous' principle of payment by tonnage.

The strike and the associated legal work presented the AWCT with a significant financial challenge, and both the National Union of Seamen and the Union of Post Office Workers helped to keep the union afloat by giving interest-free loans. However, it was still forced to make some cutbacks: some staff were made redundant while other officials agreed to accept reduced salaries.

Like other officers' organisations, the AWCT devoted a lot of its energy to the training, welfare and professionalism of its members, resisting repeated attempts by owners during the 1920s and 1930s to introduce automatic calling and alarm devices, and defending training and certification standards. It also set up residential (radio) clubs in major UK ports, run on a cooperative basis and offering 'good food and accommodation at reasonable prices'. Sadly, these were to fall victim to the slump in the shipping industry during the 1930s.

The AWCT was also active on the global front, in June 1922 organising a meeting in Brussels which established the International Federation of Radiotelegraphists. With an initial membership of organisations in 12 countries, including the Netherlands, France, Belgium and Canada, this sought to protect and improve the status of members and to secure standardised worldwide employment conditions for radiotelegraphists by establishing a uniform crewing scale and uniform working hours, on the basis of an eight-hour day.

Under an agreement with the employers in 1937, the term 'wireless operator' was replaced by 'radio officer (RO)', a title which the AWCT had long claimed on behalf of its members. Later in the year, it changed its name to the Radio Officers' Union (ROU) and affiliated to the TUC. In 1940 it expanded its membership to include shore-based inspectors and technical employees of the wireless companies. In the same year, the union joined the Officers' (Merchant Navy) Federation, and the following year took a seat at the National Maritime Board.

In the post-war period the union fought hard, nationally and internationally, to resist the removal of radio officers from aircraft and to head off shipowners' repeated attempts to reduce RO carriage requirements for ships under certain tonnage thresholds, or operating in defined areas only. In 1958 it warned of a growing retention problem linked to the lack of any right for ROs to choose the type of ship or the route they could sail on. 'The radio officer,' it asserted, 'tires of being messed around and shot from ship to ship, not to mention quick turn-rounds and curtailment of hard-earned leave'. In 1961 it said the shortages had become so acute that some large fishing vessels were sailing with no ROs, and that without action to address 'inadequate remuneration and unnecessarily onerous conditions of employment', the outlook was very bleak.

However, in 1964 the ROU secured a major victory with the adoption of a model worldwide training syllabus for radio officers. Agreed by representatives from 11 countries at a conference under the chairmanship of ROU general secretary Hugh O'Neill, the proposal aimed to ensure that global training standards should be raised and kept under constant review to meet the growing demands created by rapid advances in radio technology.

In 1967 the ROU changed its name to the Radio and Electronic Officers' Union (REOU), reflecting the technological changes in the nature of its members' work. By this time its membership had extended from the Merchant Navy to ROs serving on deep-sea fishing vessels and oil rigs, and in shore-based technical support and servicing roles. In 1970 it organised a strike of shore-based Marconi Marine technicians in support of a 20 per cent pay claim, and in the following year it staged a successful eight-week overtime ban by shore-based technicians to secure an improved pay offer from Marconi. In 1978 the union organised a successful work-to-rule of members serving on North Sea oil platforms in a dispute over Marconi's failure to fully implement the NMB pay and productivity agreement, but by now it was facing increasingly concerted pressure from shipowners seeking dispensations from the rules requiring the carriage of radio officers in certain trades. And by the 1980s technological advances began to spell the end of the 'sparky' era.

7 War and peace 1: birth of national negotiations

As seafarers became increasingly organised and more effective in their struggle to improve conditions, shipowners sought to counter their 'tyrranical'[sic] demands by forming a central association to represent their interests. In the summer of 1890 they established the Shipping Federation, partly as an attempt to head off a potential alliance between unions representing officers and ratings.

The prospect of a union representing officers and ratings prompted British owners to establish the Shipping Federation in 1890. It owned three ships to support its strike-breaking efforts, with police and strike-breakers pictured onboard the Lady Jocelyn *during the 1911 dispute.*

It expanded rapidly, opening offices in all the main ports, running strike-breaking ships, and attracting into its membership many prominent companies, including P&O, the Royal Mail Steam Packet and Shaw Savill & Albion, and, from 1902, encouraging them to carry apprentices on all suitable steamships.

Twenty-one years after the launch of the federation, its settlement of a strike by the NSFU helped to consolidate its increasing involvement in negotiations over the pay and conditions of British seafarers.

Union members had been unhappy for a long time before the dispute had begun; they had a long list of demands, including union recognition, improved and uniform pay and conditions on all ships, the fixing of hours and overtime rates, better onboard accommodation and the right for union stewards to be present at hiring sessions. They also wanted to see the abolition of degrading medical inspections in which seafarers were 'mauled about and handled as though they were a piece of New Zealand mutton'.

When the Shipping Federation rejected a request for talks, the NSFU called the strike, setting the start date as 14 June 1911. Six days before the scheduled start, seamen walked off ships in Southampton following a stoppage by coal bunkerers and trimmers working on the liner *Olympic*. Within days the dispute had spread across the country: Goole and Hull soon followed Southampton, and, thanks to the recently formed International Transport Workers' Federation, sympathy strikes ensued at ports in Belgium and the Netherlands, while German unions contributed to the strike fund. Dock workers, lightermen, scalers, coal heavers and railwaymen were quick to show support and take action in support of the seafarers. Within just a few weeks, an estimated 120,000 workers were out on strike and – even though the Shipping Federation had brought in vessels manned by strike-breakers, police and foreign crews in a concerted attempt to keep things moving – ports across the country were paralysed.

By late June 1911 the striking seafarers were wringing concessions from the owners at port after port. The first general settlement was in Hull, followed by agreements with local owners at other ports, eventually culminating with new and improved national terms set out in an overall White Book Agreement, signed and effective on 3 August.

For seafarers, the 1911 strikes left a lasting legacy – a legacy still felt today. The employers had been forced to make significant concessions, not least on the principle of union recognition and the end of the hated system in which the Shipping Federation would employ only those men who held federation tickets. There were also immediate and significant improvements in pay, with some rates for skilled seamen rising from around £4 10s a month to £9 a month.

Buoyed by the ratings' success, the officers' organisations began to draw up demands for their members. The Marine Engineers' Association had noted in July 1911 that one shipping company was paying its leading stokers £6 10s a month compared with £5 10s for junior engineer officers. Some junior engineers serving with Donaldson Line even asked whether they could be signed on as firemen, so their wages could be improved.

Managing to secure a meeting with the employers early in 1912, the masters' and officers' organisations obtained substantial pay rises for their members and also helped to finalise an agreement on the first national wage scale for seafarers hired in Britain, including non-white crewmen. However, the lascars hired overseas could still work on British ships at rates some 20 to 50 per cent below the standard.

In the first two decades of its existence the federation had made repeated claims that it was not interested in engaging in pay talks on behalf of its members and that its role was simply to maintain 'freedom of contract' between employers and employees. But in January 1912 it took part in a meeting described by the Marine Engineers' Association as 'the most important epoch in the history of shipping', with representatives from 12 shipowners' organisations sitting around the table with the MEA, the MMSA and the Sunderland Shipmasters' Association.

IMSG member Captain Charles Fryatt, executed by the German authorities in 1916 for attempting to ram a U-boat with his ferry, was a high-profile casualty of the First World War. His death provoked angry protests from the British officers' organisations, and the MMSA established a fund in his memory.

From this emerged the first form of a national pay scale for seafarers, although it would be some years before this was embraced by the industry; indeed, the strike action organised by the MEA in the summer of 1914 was a response to the failure of some owners to improve on the new rates.

It took the Great War, and the threat of the UK being starved into submission by U-boat attacks, for shipping's industrial relations to evolve to a higher level. The war, and the arrival of submarine warfare, put civilian seafarers right into the front line of conflict. Some 15 million tons of world shipping was lost – 9 million tons from the UK fleet alone – and almost 15,000 British seafarers died as a result of enemy action between 1914 and 1918.

From the outbreak of hostilities the MMSA, the IMSG and the MEA were quick to assist their members. As well as negotiating 'war risk' pay and agreements, one of the first priorities was to stop the appalling practice through which seafarers were taken off pay as soon as their ships were sunk. Although the British Admiralty agreed in 1915 to pay wages to the surviving crew of a ship under charter to the government until they reached their homes, many commercial companies showed no such compassion until 1917. That year they were forced to do so, under a Board of Trade requirement for officers and seamen on ships 'lost by war risk' to be paid one month's wages or wages up to their arrival in the UK. Even then, the MMSA had to argue for the Board of Trade to extend the arrangements to shipmasters, who had been excluded from the original scheme.

The MEA reported that some of its members had survived not one loss but as many as four, yet the unions had to spend much of their time fighting for compensation for members who had lost personal belongings when their ship had gone down; such payments were not automatic.

As part of their negotiations over 'warlike operations' service, the unions managed to get increased pay rates and pensions for seafarers serving on trading ships requisitioned for war service. The unions were also successful in securing government agreement to reduce the rates of income tax for merchant seafarers and provide assistance for their travel to and from their vessels.

The unions also provided support for members who had been interned in prisoner of war camps, sending parcels of food and clothing to them, and maintaining lines of communication. In 1914 the IMSG urged the British government to arrange an exchange of interned British, German and Austrian merchant captains and officers, and in December 1915 the MMSA launched a Christmas appeal for funds to supply gifts of provisions and warm clothing to 2,000 merchant seafarer PoWs of all ranks. The officers' organisations also worked with welfare agencies to supply clothing and footwear for seafarers coming ashore after attacks on their vessels, and to establish benevolent funds 'to relieve distress amongst members or their dependents caused by the war'.

As the war losses mounted the fragmented nature of the crewing arrangements for merchant ships presented significant challenges to the government. It had established the Ministry of Shipping in 1916 to better coordinate the supply of tonnage, and had created an interdepartmental Mercantile Marine Conciliation Committee in an attempt to ease problems with the supply of seafarers and to head off the increasing threat of disputes over such issues as pay rates and working hours.

In November 1917, following a meeting between government representatives, owners and unions, which had been convened against the background of growing demands for adequate and standard wages for all seamen, the National Maritime Board (NMB) was formed to jointly negotiate pay scales and conditions of employment binding upon shipowners. Just six days later detailed recommendations for standard national wages for seafarers were announced, with the increases backdated to 6 October.

The need to better regulate the supply of seafarers was another significant founding principle for the NMB. While the owners had spent several decades seeking to control the supply, the agreement on the NMB covered 'the consideration, regulation, and supervision of the supply, nationality, engagement, and discharge of seamen on British vessels by means of the establishment of a single source of supply jointly controlled by employers and employed'.

The union side (comprising the MMSA, IMSG, MEA, the Coastwise Masters, Mates and Engineers' Association, the NSFU and the National Union of Ship Stewards, Cooks, Butchers and Bakers) formed the Seafarers Joint Council (SJC) 'to secure unity of action … for the general improvement of all social and economic conditions of merchant seafarers'.

The NMB's existence had been intended to be temporary, for the duration of the war, but the SJC then secured an agreement with the Shipping Federation that all the decisions and issues agreed by the NMB would be maintained after its demise. So both sides resolved to maintain it after the war, independent of the government, and this body came into operation in 1920, with functions including fixing wages and conditions, supervision of the engagement of seamen, avoiding stoppages and lockouts, and discussing manning scales, leave, accommodation and welfare. It also administered the Mercantile Marine Masters & Officers' Relief Fund, which had been established in 1919 to provide financial help to masters and officers in distress as a result of sickness or unemployment.

This new structure was hailed as 'the first real experiment in industrial self-government for the shipping industry' and was credited with a dramatic improvement in industrial relations. In 1934 Board of Trade president Lord Runciman would tell Parliament: 'There is not one industry in this country which has been so free from labour disputes as the shipping industry in the last 20 years. I put that down entirely to the working of the National Maritime Board.'

In fact, the NMB's introduction had not been entirely harmonious. In July 1918, for instance, masters and officers serving on the steamers owned by the railway companies took industrial action, threatening to resign *en masse* in protest at delays in applying the NMB standard wages to their rates.

Nevertheless, in 1919 the *IMSG Gazette* noted how the war and the creation of the SJC had engendered 'a new feeling of mutual respect and understanding one for the other' within the merchant service. Keen to carry this spirit forward, the unions organised a joint seafaring conference in February 1919, with an agenda that ranged from improving pay and conditions, to working hours, to the establishment of a national pension fund for merchant seafarers, and to 'the desirability of the crewing of the Merchant Service being confined to British subjects'.

Years of lobbying by the officers' organisations finally paid off in 1918 when the government agreed to introduce a standard uniform for the Merchant Navy. The MMSA consulted members over the proposals.

The unions had emerged from the conflict with some major and lasting advances, such as helping to get seafarers included for the first time in the national unemployment insurance scheme, and the unions' war-related work went on long after peace was declared. The MMSA, IMSG and MEA were kept busy pursuing war risk compensation claims on behalf of members and their dependents, as well as reparations claims under the Treaty of Versailles. Together with ratings' representatives, they managed to secure a meeting with the prime minister, David Lloyd George, to press the case for full compensation and reparations for members who had been killed, injured or interned during the conflict. The MMSA, in particular, was collecting evidence from masters and officers about cases in which they had 'experienced outrages at the hands of the enemy … or where international laws have been broken'.

The sacrifices made by seafarers were recognised by King George V's decision to confer the title of Merchant Navy on the commercial fleet, and by the agreement in 1918 to introduce a standard merchant service uniform. This was something the unions had been seeking for some time, with the MMSA's first annual meeting hearing 60 years previously that such attire 'would add greatly to the respectability of Masters and Mates, and gain them an attention, and command respect, such as they do not now obtain'.

However, the apparent harmony created through creation of the NMB was soon to be sorely tested. A letter to the *Journal of the Marine Engineers' Association* in 1917 from one of its members had proved sadly prophetic:

> Newspapers wax eloquent nowadays on the value of the Mercantile Marine, but it required a serious crisis in the country's affairs to bring this to the notice of either press or public – clear proof that we have always been content to 'carry on' and make no fuss. A week after the war, we shall be forgotten again unless we make ourselves heard.

In 1920, only three years later, the MEA joined with all the seafarers' organisations to protest against plans to exclude shipping from the legislation that was laying down an eight-hour day in industry. 'If the general public can only be sufficiently impressed with the hardships we have endured for all time, we need have no fear of being excluded from the Bill,' the MEA journal confidently contended. The IMSG also weighed in, pointing out that there were now 20,000 unemployed British seafarers, and that an improved working time regime would help to cut these numbers. In the following year, the guild made a direct appeal to the prime minister to warn that some 3,000 masters and officers were in a 'state of destitution through want of work' and in need of practical assistance from the government.

In March 1921 the guild and the MEA loudly protested against the Shipping Federation's proposals to cut the wages of navigating and engineer officers by £4 10s a month. The owners argued that the cuts were needed because some 10 per cent of the merchant fleet was in lay-up. A brief post-war boom had seen many maritime nations making significant investments in their merchant fleets – Dutch tonnage, for instance, rose by around 60 per cent between 1919 and 1924 – and many others moved quickly to fill the gaps left by the loss of so many British ships. British owners, effectively unsubsidised, were having to compete against such state-supported fleets as those in the United States, Scandinavia, Germany and Italy. The British share of the world fleet fell from its peak of 49 per cent in 1907 to 30.9 per cent in 1924, while the growing global gap between the volume of world trade and the size of the world fleet helped to exacerbate one of the British shipping industry's periodic slumps – this one so dramatic that some freight rates fell to barely 5 per cent of the levels they had been at the height of the war.

In November 1931 talks between the Shipping Federation and the unions broke down after their failure to agree on the owners' proposals to suspend the annual leave agreement, cut pay by as much as 22 per cent for some ranks, and to reduce or remove a range of allowances. Following further negotiations, the officers' organisations managed, as in 1921, to cap the cuts to a flat rate of 10 per cent.

By 1932 more than 1.6 million tons of British shipping were laid up, and as many as 56,000 British seafarers of all grades (one-third of the workforce) were unemployed. Some shipmasters and officers resorted to serving as able seamen to stay working at sea, and their plight was highlighted by the case of one who had collapsed exhausted near St Paul's Cathedral in London after a day of walking the streets in search of work. Only third mates and fourth engineers came within the scale laid down for unemployment relief (ironically, because of the cuts in their pay rates) while officers of higher rank had to live on their savings, if they had any.

Officers' organisations called for the government and the owners to reduce the damaging surplus of seafarers by restricting the number of apprentice and cadet entrants. They argued that the lack of any central control over recruitment had helped to stoke up the 'boom and bust' employment market in which 'a general feeling of insecurity and hopelessness has permeated the Service to the great detriment of all concerned'. It was not difficult to predict the number of officers needed four years ahead, they contended, and a special panel of the NMB should be established to determine the annual total of new recruits. Such a move represented a further step towards centralisation of employment and training, consolidating a Shipping Federation scheme introduced in 1935 to set a general syllabus of education and training for future officers.

The slump in shipping had not only driven down pay and fuelled seafarer unemployment but had also served to depress working conditions. For instance, although by the 1930s officers were entitled to 14 days of annual leave, many felt unable to take it because of the risk of losing their job whilst away from their ship. And while MEA had, in the early days of the NMB, negotiated superior rates of pay for engineers on motor ships, from 1931 onwards it had to fight shipowners' moves to cut this premium.

Insecurity was fuelled by the owners' readiness to use foreign crews. In September 1934 MMSA secretary Alfred Wilson complained that things had become so bad that in the Mediterranean ships were sailing under the British flag without a single British seafarer on board; in some cases, he told the Board of Trade, the masters and officers could not speak a word of English. Calling for a new version of the Aliens Restriction Act to control foreign crewing, he warned that the red ensign had become 'the cheapest flag under which to run ships and the one which permits of the greatest freedom to commit abuses'.

Conditions on board the increasingly elderly ships in the UK fleet were often appalling. Seafarers were three times more likely to die from tuberculosis than the average British male, and almost three times more likely than a coalminer to be killed in a workplace accident. The MEA urged its members to refuse to sign on to ships 'where they would serve in surroundings which are inadequately ventilated or occupy quarters which are sufficiently spacious or well situated to allow healthy sleeping or recreative periods'.

Until the mid-1930s shipping companies did not have to provide bedding for officers, while many vessels – especially in the coastal trades – lacked bathrooms or even facilities for washing clothes. Coal-fired bogie stoves and oil and paraffin lamps were still in common use, and in 1934 the annual report from the Manchester Medical Officer of Health noted that 'these deposit a film of dirt upon everything in the compartment'. Crews on older tonnage relied on ice boxes rather than freezers for food storage, while provisions were based on scales which had been set some 30 years back, with no mention of fresh fruit and vegetables.

Not surprisingly, perhaps, these conditions were to lead to a major new development in the representation of shipmasters and officers …

8 Unity at last: the Officers' Federation and the NEOU

Captain William Coombs, founder of the Navigators' & Engineer Officers Union and the Officers' (Merchant Navy) Federation.

Standing at 4 feet 10 inches, Captain William Coombs was reported to have been the shortest man ever to hold a British master mariner's certificate. But while small in stature, he was hugely dynamic in character and tenacity, and was to have a radical impact on the representation of officers. His friend, the seafarer turned author Alan Villiers, wrote in 1957: 'I believe his name should, and will, go down in our maritime history as that of a great figure, comparable to that of Samuel Plimsoll.'

In December 1920 Captain Coombs was working in Shanghai for the Chinese Maritime Customs Service when he met another British shipmaster. Talking about life at sea and former colleagues, they discussed the way in which their careers could be abruptly terminated by the suspension or cancellation of their certificate, demonstrated by the case of a mutual acquaintance who, after his certificate had been withdrawn as a consequence of a collision, was now 'drifting around poverty corner in Fenchurch Street looking for a ship to sign on as an AB'. That evening, Coombs decided to return to England to establish an insurance scheme to give some financial protection to officers whose tickets were cancelled or suspended by the authorities following an official Board of Trade inquiry into the loss of a ship, a collision or other accident.

The Navigators & General Insurance Company (N&G) was launched barely a month after Coombs returned to the UK, and by the end of 1921 it had more than 1,000 officers on its books.

At the outset Coombs had stressed that the company was not seeking to compete with the existing officer organisations and was therefore not offering legal defence as a benefit of holding an N&G policy. However, after the MMSA and the IMSG had rebuffed his requests for cooperation and begun to offer certificate insurance to their members, he added 'legal defence' to the N&G indemnity policy, together with a directory of solicitors in major ports around the world. The rivalry became so intense that in 1930 the N&G took the IMSG to court to secure the withdrawal of the IMSG's defamatory claims that Coombs had argued in favour of wage cuts during talks with the shipowners.

N&G continued to develop its services, moving on to recover owed wages; win reinstatement for officers who had been wrongfully dismissed; and set up a new department to give income tax advice to officers, and assistance to them in finding work. It also handled hundreds of reparations claims on behalf of officers seeking damages for loss and suffering during the war.

In addition it pursued some high-profile legal cases, helping to secure the release of a Glen Line officer imprisoned without trial in Russia and of a master detained without trial in South America. It also succeeded in quashing a jail sentence imposed by a Belgian court on the master of the British ship *Australia* after he had been found guilty of involuntary manslaughter when his vessel, under pilotage in the Scheldt, had collided with and sunk another British ship, *Nautilus*.

Coombs had published a sort of manifesto in 1925 – a book entitled *The Nation's Key Men*, which he sent at his own expense to more than 9,000 officers. In it he criticised the 'failure of lack of vision' of the existing officers' organisations in providing effective representation for their members. Over 230 pages he explained the daunting scale of challenges facing shipmasters and officers – many of which would be familiar to their counterparts today – including criminalisation, commercial pressures, the high costs of training, working weeks of 84 hours, and more. The merchant service had been crucial to the UK's survival in the war, he argued, and its seafarers deserved much better.

By that time the N&G had enrolled more than 5,000 officers and was adding to this total at a rate of more than 1,200 a year. It made a series of attempts to be recognised by the National Maritime Board as a representative organisation for officers, but these were vetoed by the MMSA, the IMSG and the MEA, much of their opposition based on the N&G's cheaper membership subscriptions.

From the N&G's foundation in 1920 Coombs had planned to use any underwriting surplus to fund its work on behalf of its members. The company faced increasing demand for its legal and support services for officers and did not pay a dividend until 1936. In an attempt to widen its income base, the N&G had launched a policy for yacht and motor boat owners, and in a further effort to answer criticism that the 'insurance company' was a commercial organisation, Coombs effectively mutualised it by buying in the shares that had been issued and forming a trust.

His next move was to play the shipowners at their own game – by forming a federation in an attempt to bring diverse and competing interests together to increase their influence whilst also maintaining their individual identity and independence. Launched in 1928, the Officers' (Merchant Navy) Federation aimed to serve as an umbrella grouping through which bodies representing masters and officers in the UK and the Commonwealth could work together under a governing body representing navigators, engineers and radio officers. In April 1929 it published an 'Officers' Charter' calling for measures including increased pay, improved accommodation, better training, abolition of the two-watch system, and 'British officers for British ships'.

Later in the year Coombs had a high-profile spat with leading shipowner Sir Walter Runciman, who had complained of a shortage of junior officers caused by stricter Board of Trade examinations, which required candidates to 'stuff their heads with all sorts of useless knowledge'. Whilst not disputing a shortage, Captain Coombs argued that the problem was caused by the owners: 'The number of boys anxious to follow the sea is, fortunately for the Empire, as large as ever. The tragedy is that many, either during or shortly after their cadetship, find the pay and conditions so unattractive that they make every endeavour to haul ashore to launch out on a new career.'

Organisations representing British officers working on the coast of China and in Singapore, Australia, New Zealand and Canada were quick to join the federation, shortly followed by the Radio Officers' Union. However, there was a strong division of opinion within the Officers' Federation about the merits and demerits of joining the NMB, with particular concerns over the potential representational arrangements and inadequate negotiating machinery. However, when the shipowners proposed in 1931 to make drastic cuts in officers' pay, the federation – by then claiming to represent 11,000 officers – protested about its exclusion from the negotiations and warned that it was pressing for a Parliamentary inquiry into conditions of service in the Merchant Navy.

The MMSA, the MEA and the guild continued to block the federation's requests to join the NMB until 1934, but in February of the following year it was elected onto the navigating officers' panel in a move that was hailed by the Federation Council as 'the beginning of a new phase in Merchant Naval affairs in that for the first time, certainly since the war, the majority of certificated seafaring officers are placed together in official negotiation with the representatives of their employers'.

In 1933, in a quest to widen the sense of community amongst merchant seafarers, Captain Coombs helped to launch the Watch Ashore – an organisation to provide a network for their wives, mothers and sweethearts. It was set up by Dorothy Nelson-Ward, the wife of the Officers' Federation president Admiral Philip Nelson-Ward, and N&G company secretary Irene Vidal with the aim of providing not only a social framework for women, to ease the burdens of being on their own for long periods, but also to focus their efforts to improve the working lives of their partners.

The inaugural meeting, held at the Officers' Federation HQ on 20 February 1933, agreed to 'form a bond of mutual interest between the wives, mothers, sisters, daughters and others interested in the wellbeing of the Officer personnel of the Merchant Navy of the British Empire' and 'further promote the objects of the Officers' (MN) Federation'.

Within a year of its formation, the Watch Ashore had opened branches in Cardiff, Glasgow and Liverpool, and it went on to have, at one stage, a dozen branches in virtually all the country's major port areas. Some of its members volunteered to train as public speakers to help raise awareness of British shipping and seafarers, and others compiled lists of good accommodation near ports where they visited their husbands' ships, as well as lobbying MPs over federation issues such as annual leave and a lowered retirement age for officers.

The Watch Ashore proved particularly useful in helping to gather more than 23,000 signatures (12,554 from officers and 10,807 from members of the public, including Poet Laureate John Masefield and one shipowner) for a petition that demanded action to address the 'grave discontent' and 'considerable grounds for complaint' among MN officers, such as the lack of a proper national contributory pension scheme for the service, the lack of legal or customary rights to periods of leave, and the absence of fixed hours of duty. On 30 November 1933 the federation procured a tug, *Britannia*, to bring the petition to Parliament. Festooned with a 40-foot banner bearing the campaign message, it sailed up the Thames, cheered on by a crowd of 200 unemployed officers on London Bridge.

The petition, calling for a public inquiry into the conditions of service of Merchant Navy officers 'with special regard to training, contract of employment, leave, remuneration, unemployment and health insurance, representation, regulation, employment of uncertificated foreign officers in British ships, benevolent work and pensions', was presented to the House of Commons by Wallasey MP Lt Col John Moore-Brabazon, who told Parliament:

> The petition sets forth 13 of the chief grounds for complaint, among which are the fact that the British officers are paid at rates considerably

below those in force in ships of other European countries, that foreign officers may be employed in British ships, and that the effect of the discontent existing among the officers upon the morale of the Merchant Service is detrimental to true national interests, and that it is a matter of national importance that the causes of such discontent be investigated,.

The petition was then put before the House of Lords by Lord Howe, whose request for an inquiry into the conditions at sea was rejected on the grounds that 'the petition was on behalf of only one section of the personnel engaged in the industry' and that 'it would be a breach of policy to set up an inquiry when there was machinery of the joint industrial council type working effectively'. (The same argument – that the National Maritime Board was the appropriate body to deal with any problems relating to the wellbeing of seafarers and their conditions of service – was to be deployed in 1941 by the minister of war transport, Lord Leathers, to reject calls for a Royal Commission to establish permanent post-war improvements in recognition of the 'paramount importance of the Mercantile Marine to the national well-being, both in times of war and peace'.)

But despite the mounting evidence from the Officers' Federation showing the scale of the problems facing its members –more than 3,000 officers out of work, many described as destitute, and experienced master mariners forced to serve as deckhands, bus drivers, window cleaners and waiters to make ends meet – the petition's call for an inquiry remained unheeded.

Captain Coombs told of certain companies which had offered men work 'on condition that they secretly return a part of their wages to the company' and in October 1934 the *Hampshire Telegraph & Post* published a report highlighting the plight of many merchant seafarers at the time. Under the headline 'A War Hero on the Dole', it reported how Captain Frank Maxwell, the commander of a Q-ship which had sunk a German U-boat in 1915, had appeared in court after obtaining unemployment benefit for his wife when she was earning money by taking in lodgers. He told the court that he was out of work because of the shipping slump; he was now living in one room and had been forced to sell his sextant, his uniform and most of the 'treasures' he had collected during his voyages. His £3 fine was paid by Captain Coombs on behalf of the Officers' Federation.

The federation described the situation as a national scandal, and argued that it was wrong that so many of its members were 'on the verge of destitution' at a time when the government continued to allow UK-flagged ships to sail with foreign crews. It urged MPs to retaliate against the subsidised fleets of competing countries by paying all or part of the wages of British-certificated

The tug Britannia arrives at the Houses of Parliament in December 1931 to deliver a 12,000-signature petition protesting about the pay and conditions of MN officers.

masters and officers. However, government ministers claimed that an inquiry into MN conditions was unnecessary, as any problems should be dealt with by the NMB – and anyhow, the proportion of foreign officers serving on British ships had declined over the past 20 years.

The simmering discontent about the state of the industry saw the creation in 1934 of the Liverpool-based National Union of Merchant Service Officers. Although it was short-lived and (with a membership of 250) its application in April 1935 for affiliation to the TUC was turned down, its very existence served as a far-reaching catalyst for change.

In February 1935 the federation warned that the owners' failure to address the atrocious conditions of service was stoking up militancy amongst officers. In April it published a report warning that many masters and officers were living in dire poverty and earning less than carpenters, donkeymen and other ratings on their ships:

> The grim joke of sea-going officers' pay has endured for too long. It is contrary to tradition that qualified officers carrying immense

responsibilities should be less well paid than men serving under their command, and that masters of great ships should live in fear and trepidation of instant dismissal without redress.

In September 1935 the Federation Council agreed unanimously to organise 'the Captains, Navigating and Engineering Officers of the Merchant Navy on sound Trade Union lines' and on 1 January 1936 the foundation of the Navigators & Engineer Officers' Union (NEOU) was announced. Its rules were built around those established by the Medical Practitioners' Union, which had been founded in 1914, and membership was open to deck and engine room officers, ships' surgeons and pursers.

As with the MEA a couple of decades earlier, the concept of a union for officers had been seen by some as being at odds with their 'professional' status. However, a ballot of N&G members showed an overwhelming 97.5 per cent to be in favour of the move, and the federation's president, Admiral Philip Nelson-Ward, told the few objectors: 'Paper tigers cannot fight.' And Captain Coombs, who had previously argued that MN officers were not trade unionists 'by instinct or conviction', noted:

> The organisation of Merchant Navy Officers on conventional trade union lines is the inevitable outcome of the failure on the part of the government and the shipping industry to heed the very reasonable representations that have been made over a long period of years.
>
> Experience has shown that the mere representation of a strong case was, of itself, not sufficient to impress upon British shipowners that pay and conditions for seagoing officers were well-nigh intolerable.

In an interview about the new union, its assistant general secretary, Douglas Tennant, promised that it would work in close cooperation with the National Union of Seamen, and its immediate objective would be to secure conditions for seafarers that were comparable with modern standards of living ashore: 'Our primary object will be to insist that merchant officers and engineers shall receive as a right, adequate pay, reasonable leave, security of a pension scheme, and just, humane and modern conditions of service. We do not contemplate the use of the strike weapon, but must remember that that is the ultimate argument.'

During its first year of existence the union attracted a total of 9,456 members (almost 5,000 of whom had been transferred N&G policyholders) and, despite the opposition of the Amalgamated Engineering Union, became affiliated to the TUC. The union set a short but ambitious set of immediate policy objectives, including a 25 per cent increase in salaries to ensure that officers' pay 'shall be commensurate with the responsibilities and duties', the right to 30 days of annual leave, total abolition of the two-watch system, abolition of engineer officers' 'field days', and overtime payments for all hours of duty in excess of 48 per week.

The early agenda was dominated by the drive to establish the Merchant Navy Officers' Pension Fund (MNOPF) – something that had been the target for its predecessors over many decades. Although some individual companies had their own schemes, the unions argued that the lack of an industry-wide scheme based on salary and length of service for all officers was 'a serious drawback to a sea career'. The Officers' Federation had developed the details of a proposed scheme in 1931 after carrying out extensive research, and in 1935, as soon as it had secured its place on the NMB, it officially submitted the proposals to the owners. In March 1936 the owners agreed in principle to a contributory pension scheme, with a working party of owners and union reps created to thrash out the details. The pension trust deed was signed at the NMB on 29 October 1937. By the end of the year, 340 companies had accepted the terms of the fund, and around 5,000 application forms had been submitted by officers.

To enable the scheme to go ahead, Parliament had to pass special regulations to reverse 1894 Merchant Shipping legislation outlawing deductions from seafarers' pay. The union wanted to ensure that officers could contribute to their pension rights wherever they were serving, and could carry them from one ship to another – an important reform, which it achieved when the scheme came into effect in January 1938.

The composition of the scheme was something of a trailblazer, with the trustees and committee of management made up of equal numbers of representatives from the officers' organisations and the shipowners. Benefits laid down by the scheme – which was governed by equal representation from participating employers and

The agreement to establish the Merchant Navy Officers' Pension Fund is signed by Sir Arthur Cauty, joint chairman of the National Maritime Board, on 29 October 1937, closely watched by NEOU general secretary William Coombs, on his left-hand side.

officers' unions – included a pension payable from the age of 65, with an early retirement option at 60.

The seemingly perennial problem of excessive hours was also in the union's sights from the outset, and it quickly flagged up its determination to secure the abolition of the two-watch system. 'We consider it is not untrue to describe our service today as utterly weary and depressed by excessive hours in port and at sea, and disgruntled to a degree on account of the paucity of time off in home ports,' it stated in January 1937. 'Stories of 70, 80, and even over 100 hours a week consistently worked are not the exception but rather the rule.'

Later in the same year the union called for an inquiry into conditions of service in the UK coastal trades, warning that officers' hours in the sector were averaging more than 80 a week, and in exceptional cases were running at 120 hours or more. Many members in the sector were denied annual leave entitlements, the NEOU argued, and those who did take time off often did so on an uncertain basis, not knowing when they would be recalled, or whether they would be replaced by an out-of-work seafarer. Conditions in the coastal fleet were akin to 'deplorable slums', it argued, and the lack of cooks on many ships, and the abysmal quality of food on board, were to blame for high levels of ill health.

The NEOU urged the government to intervene to help the British coastal fleet compete against foreign operators, along the lines of the British Shipping (Assistance) Act of 1935, which had given owners of tramp ships up to £10 million to modernise the fleet through a 'scrap and build' programme. It also argued that 'no foreign vessels should be allowed to trade on our coasts unless their pay and conditions are equivalent to those granted under revised British agreements'.

The union was also actively highlighting concerns about safety at sea, with evidence to show that standards of seaworthiness were lamentable on an alarming number of British vessels. It had campaigned for full inquiries into four losses which had cost the lives of almost 100 British seafarers, including the 1934 foundering of the tanker *La Crescenta* (which, it was revealed, had suffered from systematic overloading) and said the findings had underlined the 'disgraceful state of affairs' within the shipping industry.

The NEOU raised alarm over incidents that suggested 'some modern ships, under certain conditions of loading, may be lacking in longitudinal structural strength', while its concerns about undermanning had been echoed in a number of accident investigation reports, and were also discussed in Parliament: the 'scandalous state of affairs' was discussed in Parliament in May 1936, when the Labour MP Arthur Greenwood quoted from the annual report of the Officers' Federation, which stated:

> During the period under review we have seen a number of reports from officers in tramp steamers complaining of steady deterioration in conditions aboard their ships. It would appear that there is a growing custom under which navigating officers, and in some cases masters, find it necessary to do manual work about the decks in order that the owners' requirements as to general upkeep (with a minimum of expenditure on shore labour) shall be met. A number of cases have been reported to us in which the man at the wheel is left in charge of the bridge, with instructions to call the officer of the watch (working about the deck) with a whistle.

On many ships the crew accommodation was situated in the forecastle, leading to horrific loss of life in collisions, and unions were pressing the Board of Trade to prohibit such arrangements.

Through the Officers' Federation, the NEOU also campaigned for better support to be given to the families of seafarers lost at sea, urging the creation of a national fund to provide pensions and allowances for widows and dependents.

Recruitment and qualifications were also high on the agenda, with the union criticising proposals put forward by the shipowners in 1935 for changes to the system of officer training – noting with regret the low educational standards sought by companies, as well as their failure to recognise 'the need for reasonable control of entry into an overcrowded service'.

However, from the middle of the decade onwards the gradual recovery of shipping markets helped the unions to claw back pay cuts and restore lost benefits. By May 1937 the NEOU was able to deliver a sort of 'never had it so good' message to members – noting that 'never before had the "time lag" twixt improved trade and improved conditions for Officers been so short'.

In the same year, the government finally moved to tackle the scandalous state of so much seafarer accommodation, passing new regulations that stopped crew quarters from being placed forward or below the load waterline except on very small vessels, and improving standards of lighting, heating, insulation and ventilation. For the first time, the comfort of seafarers was made a specific requirement, and plans for crew quarters had to be submitted to the Board of Trade for approval. However, there was still a need for the NEOU to continue to campaign loudly in protest against the British government's failure to ratify international conventions relating to the regulation of hours of duty and crewing, and the slow progress towards legislation outlawing the use of uncertificated officers in home trade vessels. The NEOU was also highly critical of the way in which British shipowners at the International Maritime Conference had voted against the proposed conventions to limit officers' hours, to set a minimum of 12 days of paid annual leave for all masters and officers, and to require all masters and navigating and engineer watchkeeping officers on ships over 200 gt to be duly certificated.

In 1936 the union published pamphlets that sought to raise awareness about the shocking working conditions endured by many members. It said that masters and officers often faced pressure 'to do wrongful things, for example overloading and falsification of logbooks' while also experiencing underpayment in contravention of agreements; it told, too, of apprentices having to sleep in the master's bath to make room for passengers. It described how first mates and second engineers in coastal ships were earning £3 15s 6d a week 'in return for strenuous and harassing work, often amounting to 100 hours a week, no study pay, no sick pay, no compensation for Saturdays and Sundays at sea, and leave virtually non-existent'.

Captain Coombs was also pressing the case for further unity, complaining about the waste of time, money and effort arising from divided representation. 'Until there is one strong officers' organisation in this country,' he warned, 'the task of securing improved conditions will be greatly hampered.' One step towards his vision had been taken on 31 March 1936, when the MMSA and the IMSG amalgamated after a number of years in which they had worked increasingly closely, jointly organising a petition to Parliament in 1931, protesting against proposed changes to helm orders, and successfully lobbying for concessionary rail fares for ships' officers. It was the MMSA that re-incorporated the guild, even though the latter had more members. In announcing the merger, the two organisations stated that the 'paramount reason' was the desire to end a division which had 'seriously retarded' efforts to improve the conditions of masters and officers and that 'the complete unification of their efforts' would 'go a long way in furtherance of the general well-being of the officers of the Merchant Navy'.

Claiming that the amalgamation amounted to 'a new era in the history of professional representation for Merchant Navy officers', they also placed some clear blue water between themselves and the NEOU by arguing that shipmasters and officers were 'members of a profession, not a trade'. And in an even more direct challenge to the NEOU, they asserted: 'The time has arrived when officers must make up their minds whether they desire a professional organisation to represent their interests, or a trade union.'

Despite such thinly veiled hostility, further progress towards collaboration was made in 1942 in an agreement 'to ensure full and complete co-operation' between the MMSA and the NEOU, and to put an end to 'pointless competition between the organisations for the enrolment of new members'. Under the terms of the agreement, the MMSA joined the Officers' Federation and confined its membership to masters serving in command. Although it maintained its autonomy, the MMSA agreed to share its district offices around the UK with the NEOU, and from that point consultation and cooperation between the officers' organisations intensified. Announcing the agreement in a joint statement, Captain Coombs and MMSA General Secretary Alfred Wilson hailed it as 'a very important step forward towards the complete realisation of the general desire that all Merchant Navy officers' organisations may work together in a spirit of complete cooperation'.

9 Federation: a long-standing global vision

Shipping is an inherently international industry, and the need for global cooperation has run strongly through the work of the maritime unions. British seafarers' complaints about being undercut by lower-cost foreign labour stretch back more than 200 years, and they accelerated sharply in 1849, when the long-standing requirements for three-quarters of a British ship's crew to be British were abolished. The disquiet was summed up by a letter from a seafarer to the *Nautical Magazine* in 1854, complaining that British shipowners had been 'forced into a most unjust and uncalled for competition with foreigners, that has so screwed him down that he is compelled to send his ships to sea at the starvation point, and obliged to carry on a system of under-manning and defective outfit that is perfectly appalling'.

In 1896 the International Federation of Ship, Dock and River Workers was created, changing its name just two years later to the International Transport Workers' Federation (ITF). Its founders had the stated aim to 'establish, so far as may be possible, a uniform rate of pay for the same class of worker in all ports and to establish a recognised working day and other regulations in the ports of the world'. They wanted to see 'a steady levelling up' of pay, in part to address shipowners' complaints that British workers were paid well in excess of those on the Continent.

Conscious of the owners' abilities to play off one national group against another, seafarers' organisations had been seeking for some time to secure international machinery to govern maritime labour issues. The creation of the International Labour Organization (ILO) in 1919 offered just such an opportunity – and in some dedicated maritime sessions of its International Labour Conference, seafarers were successful in making the case for 'the very special questions concerning the minimum conditions to be accorded to seamen' to be dealt with on a separate basis.; in 1920 the International Labour Office agreed to the creation of a maritime section and a Joint Maritime Commission (JMC), consisting of equal numbers of seafarer and shipowner representatives.

Before the ILO had held that first conference in Washington in autumn 1919, UK seafaring unions had presented the British government's delegate to the meeting with a 15-point programme of demands covering such things as the minimum wage, working hours, manning scales, food and accommodation, compulsory pilotage, wireless telegraphy services and loadlines, and banning or limiting deck cargoes.

Earlier that year the MMSA, IMSG and MEA had taken part in two international maritime union conferences – one in London, one in Paris – which sought to shape the ILO agenda. The London meeting, which had been organised by the recently formed International Seafarers' Federation (ISF), noted the scale of shipping losses during the Great War, and unanimously agreed a motion calling for 'adequate and full reparation and compensation for the crimes committed on seafarers of all classes'. The motion was ratified by the subsequent International Seamen's Congress in Paris, where the UK delegates, along with representatives from the United States, Denmark, France, Italy, Norway and Sweden, agreed to a demand that at least £1,000 compensation should be paid to the family 'of every seafarer who was a victim of German crimes during the war'.

The Paris meeting also discussed the details of a proposed minimum wage for seafarers, which was intended to be progressed at the first ILO maritime session in June 1920, together with demands for an 8-hour day and a 48-hour working week at sea. Ahead of this meeting the ISF convened a preparatory 'international conference of seafarers' in Genoa in an attempt to 'make it possible for the world's merchant seaman to present a solid front to the League of Nations meeting'. This was attended by some 75 delegates from countries including the UK, the Netherlands, Belgium, France, Germany, Greece, Italy, Japan, Norway, Spain and Sweden.

Delegates from the MMSA and IMSG attended the subsequent ILO meeting in the role of technical advisers, with MEA General Secretary David Bramah serving as one of the British workers' representatives. The conference came painfully close to agreement on a convention to limit working hours in line with the unions' demands, and the MMSA, IMSG and MEA jointly pushed the UK government to put the subject of shorter hours for seafarers on the agenda of the ILO's 1928 maritime conference – but it

Delegates from the MMSA, IMSG and MEA took part in a conference in Paris in 1919 to discuss the agenda for the International Labour Organization's first Joint Maritime Commission – including proposals to set a global minimum wage for seafarers.

would not be until 1936 and the passing of Convention 57 on the hours of work and manning at sea that international regulation of working time was eventually agreed. However, in 1928 the unions – who had been making the case for an International Seamen's Code, to provide a 'uniform law' for the world's seafarers – were successful in securing the adoption of three conventions, covering: the establishment of facilities for finding employment for seamen; the fixing of the minimum age for admission of children to employment at sea; and the provision of unemployment indemnity in case of loss or foundering of the ship.

The sheer scale of the British Empire meant that British masters and officers worked across the globe, and from an early stage both the MMSA and the IMSG had strong relationships with such organisations as the Australian Merchant Service Guild and the China Coast Officers' Guild. In 1899 the IMSG expressed solidarity with officers serving in the British India Steam Navigation Company, who had taken successful strike action over pay and leave in the previous year.

The Officers' (MN) Federation had been created by Captain Coombs to represent members across the Commonwealth, and in December 1938 he visited India in an attempt to improve conditions for officers serving on the Indian coast and to explore the possibility of opening an NEOU office in the country. However, this failed to get off the ground because of differences over the gap between pay rates for British and Indian officers.

In January 1936 the Officers' Federation affiliated with the International Mercantile Marine Officers' Association (IMMOA) which had been established in 1925 by Dutch, Belgian, French and Scandinavian officers to 'defend and safeguard the interests of mercantile marine officers, and to foster the ties of friendship and cooperation between organisations of mercantile marine officers of all nations'. IMMOA's core aim was to provide an effective voice for officers at the ILO, and in 1932 discussions about the possible affiliation of the Officers' Federation had begun against a background of fears that European shipowners were making concerted attempts to cut the pay of officers.

The federation rapidly became an active member of the IMMOA, with Captain Coombs elected to the post of president in 1937. He soon gave particularly strong support to its efforts to secure a global agreement to reduce the threat of criminalisation by reserving criminal jurisdiction in collision cases to the country of the vessel's flag. Stressing the importance of such work, Coombs told NEOU members: 'We have long recognised that your well-being is inseparably linked up with the well-being of ships' officers the world over and that we cannot do our job on your behalf properly if we fail to realise that shipping is essentially an international industry.'

This booklet celebrated the success of the cooperation between officers' unions during the Second World War, with the Officers' (MN) Federation hosting representatives from more than 30 officers' unions from countries which had been invaded by Germany.

In October 1936, the NEOU took part in the ILO's Joint Maritime Conference in Geneva, which discussed proposals for six new conventions – including hours and manning, holidays with pay, minimum professional qualifications and sickness insurance – as well as a recommendation on seafarers' welfare in ports. The union lobbied strongly for the UK to implement these measures, and former ILO director Sir Harold Butler wrote in 1939 that 'it is curious to note that Great Britain is behind countries like Australia, Belgium, Sweden and the United States in adopting the international standard of hours and manning at a time when complaints are constantly heard that enough men cannot be induced to go to sea'.

Early in the Second World War the Officers' Federation took over the administration of more than 30 officers' unions from Allied countries which had been invaded by Germany – a task which was transferred to the IMMOA in May 1941 when, following the German invasion of Belgium, it switched its headquarters from Antwerp to London. Both the Federation and the IMMOA were involved in the considerable work to establish the necessary negotiating machinery in London to enable discussions over the pay and conditions of the Allied unions.

In 1942 the ILO managed to convene a JMC meeting in London, with the intention of discussing progress on the conventions agreed in 1936 and the impact of war on merchant seafarers. However, the maritime unions wanted to look further ahead, and the IMMOA worked with the ITF to revive the concept of an International Seafarers' Charter, setting out minimum standards and 'best practicable social legislation' for seafarers of all nationalities. The IMMOA and the ITF were both determined to ensure that the horrific wartime sacrifices of seafarers were not in vain, and that in peacetime 'seafarers would not be pawns in any effort made by owners to cut one another's throats'. Likewise, the Officers' Federation had voiced its worries that shipowners' predictions of a peacetime return to 'free competition' would in practice mean a return to 'cut-throat competition in operating costs' and 'a return to the insecurity and miseries of the inter-war years'.

The charter displayed a clear and far-sighted recognition of the need to organise globally in an inherently international industry:

> During the period between the two world wars it was clearly demonstrated that socially progressive countries, where disposed to raise the standards of the shipping industry, were seriously handicapped by the weakening it involved in the competitive power of their national merchant navies. From this it follows that the international character of the shipping industry makes it imperative to seek the widest possible uniformity in the working conditions of the seafarers, as otherwise the standards of the most advanced countries will always be endangered by those of the countries lagging behind.

The charter was also significant in the way it galvanised an unprecedented level of cooperation between the ratings' and the officers' unions. Powered by a strong sense of common purpose and a passionate desire to build a better future for members, they worked together to develop the proposals over the following two years; the final document was adopted in July 1944 at a conference of seafarers' unions from 12 countries (including the UK, the Netherlands, Greece, China and India).

The charter was made up of 11 sections including: wages and the important principle of an internationally common minimum wage; allowances and bonuses; continuous employment; entry, training and promotion; hours and manning; accommodation; hygiene and medical services; safety; social insurance; full recognition of seafarers' organisations; and the legal rights and obligations of seafarers.

The charter was bold in its ambitions, arguing that an international minimum wage was justified on the grounds that seafarers 'perform the same work and spend a considerable part of their earnings outside their own country in foreign currency'. Instead of the 'distasteful' debasement of seafarers' pay and conditions to meet 'foreign competition', the charter contended that a global minimum wage would force owners to compete 'wholesomely among themselves – in ship design, in economical management and administration, in enterprise and in adventure'. It also sought to put an end to the impermanence of seafaring work by stopping the system under which employment was terminated at the end of a voyage.

In turn, these proposals helped to shape the agenda of a special ILO maritime conference held in Seattle in 1946, which adopted nine conventions and four recommendations drawing from the charter, and dealing with such items as wages, hours of work and manning, pensions and social security, crew accommodation, food and catering, and holidays with pay. Opposition from shipowners and governments had seen off some of the most ambitious elements of the charter – but, as NEOU general secretary Douglas Tennant told the union's 1946 AGM, the unions 'got a good deal more than the shipowners wished to give'. Just over a decade later, as he announced a review of the extent to which the charter's principles had been adopted, he was able to argue that it had 'undoubtedly influenced national negotiations in practically every maritime country, with the result that there probably is today greater uniformity of basic conditions of employment than at any time hitherto'.

From 1936 the increasingly close relationship between the ITF and IMMOA resulted in a series of proposals for amalgamation or affiliation. With IMMOA operating from the NEOU's London offices during the war, it was agreed in autumn 1940 that Captain Coombs and IMMOA Secretary-Treasurer Omer Becu should begin discussions with the ITF on the proposals. By December 1944 agreement had been reached for IMMOA to affiliate to the ITF's Seafarers' Section and to be part of a new ITF sub-section for officers, on an equal footing with the ratings. An emergency meeting of IMMOA's executive committee in London finalised arrangements for the closure of the US office and agreed to hold talks with the ITF in advance of the 1945 ILO maritime conference. In the following year, delegates to the 11th IMMOA Congress, held in Zurich, voted by 24 to 3, with 10 abstentions, to affiliate to the ITF on condition that a special officers' section be created.

As former ITF general secretary Harold Lewis wrote in his thesis covering the ITF's turbulent years between 1945 and 1965:

> The bringing together of officers' and ratings' unions, of 'white collar' and 'blue-collar' seafarers, had great symbolic and practical significance. Symbolically, it illustrated how the war had shaken and reshaped some of the old class distinctions; practically, it reduced greatly the shipowners' ability to play one group off against the other.

On a national level, the build-up to the war during the later 1930s had led to increased cooperation between the British officers' and ratings' unions. Once again, merchant ships and their crews had found themselves in the firing line as the Spanish civil war intensified. Between July 1936 and April 1939 at least 35 British seafarers were killed and 29 British merchant ships sunk or lost, with more than 50 blockade-runners being bombed from the air, 2 damaged by mines, 5 attacked by submarines and 23 seized or detained by Franco's forces. The Officers' Federation had pressed owners over the legal liabilities for masters and officers killed and injured in these attacks, urging them to ensure that arrangements were in place to provide proper compensation.

In the face of government indifference to the attacks, the Officers' Federation and the National Union of Seamen (NUS) worked with the Progressive Film Institute to produce a 16-minute documentary – *Britain Expects* – to be shown to cinema audiences. This vividly highlighted the risks that seafarers were facing, stressed the scale of the UK's dependence upon shipping for supplies of food and raw materials, and accused Neville Chamberlain of being the first British prime minister to deny the Merchant Navy adequate protection. While the film was banned by the British Board of Film Censors, because of sensitivities about criticism of the government's appeasement policies, the unions' warnings were to be dramatically underscored over the next six years.

10   War and peace 2: building back better

It is hard to overstate the scale of the sacrifice made by merchant seafarers in the Second World War. More than 32,000 lost their lives as a direct result of enemy action – around one in every four men in the Merchant Navy at the start of the war – and the MN mortality rate was higher than that in any of the armed forces. On some convoys more than 60 per cent of all ships were lost, while many seafarers had multiple experiences of serving on ships that were sunk by torpedoes.

In the immediate years before the war the NEOU had been warning the government about the strategic importance of shipping and seafaring. In September 1936, as the British government embarked upon a policy of rearmament, the Officers' Federation warned that 'there were few indications that the authorities were sufficiently mindful of the importance of the Merchant Navy as an integral part of the defence of the Empire'. Noting the impact of submarine attacks in the First World War, the federation called for merchant seafarers to be given specialist training in the self-defence of their vessels. In the months before the war began, the MMSA called for seamen to be given proper training in boat-work but, as maritime academic and former seafarer Tony Lane noted, 'the government's response, soon to be tragically proved wrong-headed, was that arrangements in place were adequate'.

In the build-up to war, Captain Coombs described how thousands of officers and ratings 'felt aggrieved with their conditions of service; many of those who were able to do so had abandoned their chosen career in disgust, with the result that there existed a serious shortage of qualified engineer officers, of junior navigating officers, and incidentally of well-trained, well-disciplined seamen'. In the face of these concerns, a Merchant Navy Reserve was set up in 1938 to create a register of experienced seafarers willing to return to sea at a time of national crisis.

The union had campaigned strongly during 1938 against the 'suicidal' proposals to lay up British ships in response to a slump in trade, warning ministers that 'the Merchant Navy is still our first and last line of defence' and pointing out that the UK's share of world tonnage had fallen from 44 per cent in 1914 to 28 per cent in 1938. Its long-standing calls for the creation of a Ministry of Shipping were hastily acted upon soon after the war broke out, and the federation, the MMSA, the MEA, the ROU and the NUS were made members of an industry-wide advisory council for the new minister, Sir John Gilmour.

The industry had worked together to develop a programme of emergency preparations, including special training, and scheduling seafaring as a 'reserved occupation'. In 1940, as the impact of war started to hit shipping hard, the owners and the unions jointly developed proposals for an 'essential work' order in an attempt to reduce the risk of ships being delayed by crew shortages. Introduced in May 1941, this had the effect of creating continuous, rather than casual, employment through a pool of reserve seafarers managed by unions, owners and the Ministry of War Transport. This centralisation of supply was highly successful, with the pool supplying an average of 400 officers and 3,250 ratings every week.

The unions also secured an agreement to which the shipowners and the Board of Trade were parties, under which shipwrecked seafarers were to get full wages – including £5 per month war risk payments – until their return to the UK or until offered another job. The NEOU had strongly opposed the use of the term 'war risk bonus' to describe these payments, arguing that seafarers were owed 'a long overdue increase in pay as it was'. Under the agreement, seafarers would also be entitled to 14 days of special shipwreck leave on full pay after returning home, in addition to any normal leave due. The NEOU welcomed, in addition, 'the speedy introduction of a scheme of disablement and widows' pensions', as well as an agreement to provide reduced rail fares for MN seafarers and their wives.

It was not until January 1943 – by which time, as it turned out, 80 per cent of all the merchant ships sunk in the war had been lost – that the Ministry of War Transport finally provided detailed advice on survival. In the interim, the union had produced 7,600 waterproof 'shipwrecked mariners' charts' of the North Atlantic to help survivors navigate their lifeboats to a point where they would be most likely to be picked up.

Soon after the war broke out, the NEOU established a secondary head office in Captain Coombs's house in Norfolk, sending a duplicate set of records and 20 clerical staff to the building. The wisdom of this was borne out on 10 May 1941, when the head office in London's Leadenhall Street was destroyed in an air raid.

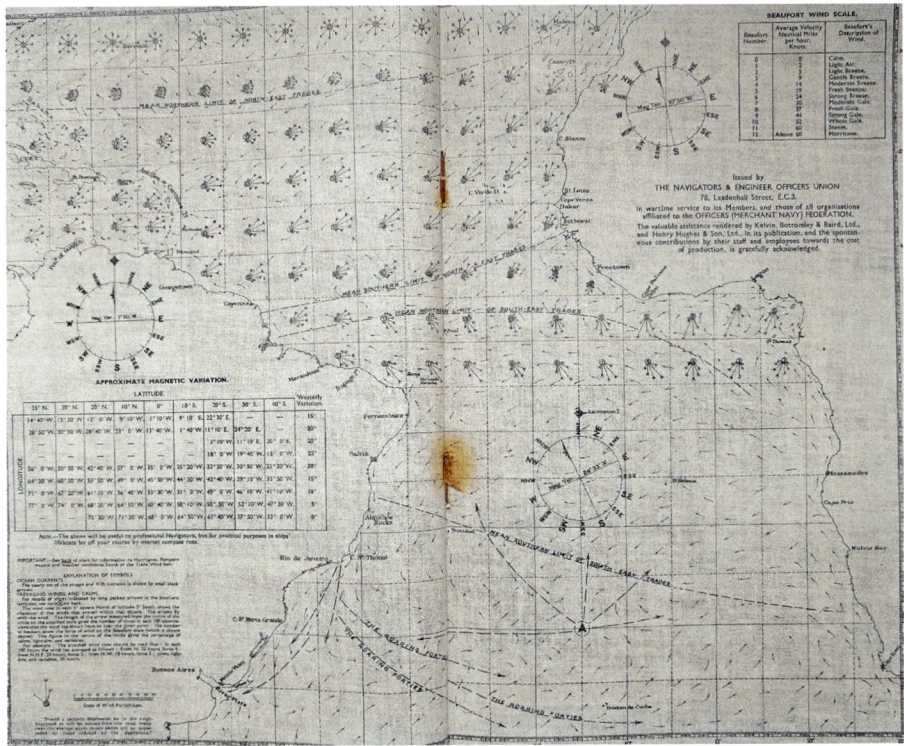

The NEOU produced more than 7,500 copies of a special waterproof chart during the Second World War to help members forced to abandon ship during the Atlantic convoys.

In true stiff upper lip spirit, however, the union managed to re-establish itself in new offices elsewhere in the same road within the space of just 48 hours. The union had also suffered the loss of its district offices in Liverpool and Avonmouth during air raids early in the same year.

Following the invasion of Norway and Denmark, the Officers' Federation cooperated with the British government in a broadcast message appealing to the masters of Danish and Norwegian ships to take their vessels to Allied ports 'with the utmost despatch'. A special coordination committee, involving representatives from the federation, the National Union of Seamen and the Norwegian Seamen's Union, was quickly established, and the federation went on to assist in the management of 18 foreign officers' unions, including those from the Netherlands, Norway, Denmark, Belgium and France, as well as, following the Japanese invasions of Hong Kong, Singapore and Shanghai, looking after the interests of the China Coast Officers' Guild and the Straits Merchant Service

Guild. The federation successfully argued against proposals to reduce the higher pay of foreign officers to British levels and to bring up any lower rates to British standards. Following talks at the National Maritime Board, the unions secured an agreement in January 1941 for a differential payment of £2 a month to be paid to British seafarers to reflect the fact that many other Allied crews were on higher rates.

After the invasion of Norway and Denmark in April 1940 and the invasion of Holland, Belgium and France in May and June of the same year, the NEOU, through the Officers' (MN) Federation, also helped to host the International Mercantile Marine Officers' Association (IMMOA) following its exile to London. With his characteristic energy, Captain Coombs travelled to New York early in 1941 to establish a US office for IMMOA to serve as a platform for its work on behalf of British, Dutch, Danish, Norwegian, Belgian, Free French and Polish officers making the dangerous Atlantic crossings. The federation also assisted in the expansion of IMMOA during the war, helping with the formation of unions for Polish and Estonian officers, as well as the admission into membership of unions representing Greek masters and navigating officers.

In 1941, in a somewhat uncanny echo of the circumstances in which the MMSA had been set up, the NEOU protested to the Ministry of War Transport over its 'arbitrary' decision to suspend the certificate of a member who had appeared before a court martial after the stranding of a naval vessel on which he was serving. The union pointed out that there was no right of appeal against the ministry's decision, although it did manage to secure the reinstatement of the officer's certificate.

In another case, the union stepped in to prevent the prosecution of a shipmaster member who had been accused of breaching regulations by having a ship that was 'inadequately staffed' for air raid protection purposes.

The NEOU also provided legal representation for the master of the cargo ship *Radchurch*, which had been carrying an iron ore cargo for the Ministry of War Transport, after he was accused of incompetence arising from the alleged premature abandonment of the vessel when the convoy it was sailing in was attacked by U-boats. The union successfully appealed against the decision to suspend the master's certificate for nine months, the court then stating that the master had been justified in giving the order to abandon ship.

Both the NEOU and the MMSA continued to complain bitterly about the poor representation of shipmasters on the National Maritime Board at this time. Companies argued that masters' conditions of employment should be the subject of private and individual negotiation, reflecting their special position as agents of the owners. But the unions contended that while many masters were serving with no written contract, some were holding letters of appointment written up to 15 years previously stating that their position was temporary, and yet others were working on the clear understanding that their services could be dispensed with at any time without notice.

Even at the height of the war the NEOU was continuing to seek action to improve conditions in the coastal fleet. The public scandal of the peacetime undermanning had become more acute during conflict, it warned, and there was a pressing need for regulations on the minimum number of crew required on coastwise vessels. In 1942 it complained that on coastwise ships the ratings, eligible for overtime payments, were often being paid more than the officers, who received no overtime for the long hours they were spending on fire-watching.

As early as October 1941 the union was turning its mind to the legacy of the war for the merchant fleet. In an article in *The Merchant Navy Journal*, Captain Coombs argued that 'national honour and inherent sense of social justice demand that after a long history of service and sacrifice culminating in a record of superb achievement during two wars, officers and seamen of Britain's Merchant Navy should have generous conditions of employment'. In 1943 assistant general secretary Douglas Tennant told the MMSA annual meeting in Liverpool that the wartime courage and sacrifice of seafarers should not be in vain, and that efforts should be directed towards securing continuity of employment, decent working conditions, action to address excessive working hours, and research into the diseases to which seafarers were particularly exposed.

During the war the Officers' Federation had sought special arrangements for the care of merchant seafarers whose physical or mental wellbeing had been damaged as a result of their service. It had also lobbied the Ministry of War Transport on behalf of members who had been held in prisoner of war camps – notably protesting about the policy that resulted in war risk payments being stopped from the moment they had been taken prisoner. In 1942 the NEOU took up the case of MN PoWs who had raised concerns that poor lighting and vitamin deficiencies could cause long-term damage to their eyesight, potentially preventing their eventual return to sea. The union pressed the Ministry of War Transport for assurances that any seafarers adversely affected in this way would be treated as suffering a war injury.

At the end of the war, the Officers' Federation was actively involved in the arrangements for the repatriation and reception of seafarers from PoW camps by ensuring, with the speedy issue of identity cards, clothing coupons, ration cards, and allowances for loss of personal effects, that they could return home as soon as possible.

The NEOU had also called for special pension arrangements to be made for

More than 4,000 British merchant seafarers were held as prisoners of war during the Second World War. Most were detained at the MILAG (Marine Internierten Lager) camp near Bremen, which was liberated in April 1945.

senior officers who had served in both world wars, allowing them to retire on an adequate pension from the age of 55.

Although seafarers suffered many appalling deprivations, the war also saw some crucial advances being made in their terms and conditions. These included measures to better control working hours for some crew, by establishing the principle of an eight-hour day in port and a nine-hour day at sea, together with the introduction of a minimum of eight weeks' pay for officers studying for higher certificates. Leave for members in the foreign-going trades rose from 14 days a year in 1936 to 2½ days per month (so, 30 days per year) in 1946, and sick pay of up to eight weeks a year was introduced.

Unions also made progress on the organisation of catering departments and improved compensation for loss of effects. The statutory victualling scale – which dated back to 1906 – was radically amended in 1940, introducing new requirements for fresh food.

The successful introduction of the Central Board for the Training of Officers for the Merchant Service in 1935 was followed, in February 1942, by its expansion to the Merchant Navy Training Board, with unions, shipowners and government representatives sitting down to draw up post-war training schemes for MN personnel. The NEOU particularly welcomed the introduction of the principle of selection and control of entrants, as well as higher entry standards for engineer officers.

The NEOU also made important advances towards improved standards of shipboard accommodation. The union had long complained that the position of trimming hatches and other freight-earning considerations were being prioritised over the size and location of cabins, and early in the war it protested about the unsatisfactory accommodation on ships being built under the Ministry of War Transport's emergency programme. The ministry responded positively to these concerns, and the union secured a National Maritime Board agreement that the ensuing improved standards should continue to apply until the 1937 instructions to surveyors were revised. The NEOU also played a major part in the drafting of an ILO convention on international minimum standards for accommodation, which was put forward at the 1946 maritime conference.

Acting on the 1936 ILO recommendations on seafarer welfare, Ernest Bevin – minister of labour and national service – established a Seamen's Welfare Board in 1940, with a core duty to set up facilities of a standard equivalent to those for shore-based industries. Welcoming this decision, the NEOU noted that seafarer welfare had traditionally been left to charities:

> There is a growing feeling, however, that there is no valid reason why seafarers should be regarded necessarily as 'objects of charity'. Officers resent the multiplicity of charitable appeals which have been made on behalf of seafarers and contend that these appeals – some of them spectacular in nature and misleading to the public – tend to create an impression in the public mind that seafarers need charity and, also, they object to being singled out as a section of the community which needs special spiritual uplift.

In November 1943 the NEOU was part of a special committee established by the government to investigate welfare provision for seafarers. The committee's report noted that maritime welfare services had traditionally been almost entirely undertaken by charities. However, since the UK's adoption of the ILO's 1936 recommendation on the Promotion of Seamen's Welfare in Ports, the committee accepted the moves toward 'a comprehensive and coordinated welfare service' for seafarers. From its recommendations the Merchant Navy Welfare Board and its related system of port or regional welfare committees was established in 1948.

In a further advance, a Merchant Navy Established Service Scheme was introduced in 1947 in an attempt to extend the degree of security and an element of career progression that had been introduced by the wartime continuity of employment arrangements.

In 1941, at the height of the Battle of the Atlantic, the writer and broadcaster J.B. Priestley made a passionate appeal on behalf of merchant seafarers:

> We owe them something more than sentimental speeches made at a time when our lives depend on their skill and courage. We owe these men a square deal. In the last war we praised them to the skies, gave them a pat on the back, and stood them drinks. What we didn't stand them were better conditions and a reasonably secure future. If we're proud of the Merchant Service now, let's see to it that we remain proud of it – and that it's something to be proud of – in the years to come.'

In the following year the Ministry of War Transport invited the Officers' Federation to submit proposals for a post-war shipping policy. The Federation Council replied that the scope of matters to be considered – including improved pay and conditions for masters and officers – meant that detailed plans would take some time to produce. However, it stressed, high priority should be placed upon the UK ratification of ILO conventions.

The NEOU repeatedly expressed hopes that the post-war period would witness a 'fundamental and spectacular revision of the whole position of seafarers in the scheme of the world's life'. Arguing that the public would be prepared to pay an extra farthing for a loaf of bread if they knew it would ensure decent pay and conditions for seafarers, it pointed out that few would notice 'the difference in cost between giving seafarers an impoverished mode of life, wretched conditions, little or no welfare amenities in ports, or, on the other hand, rewarding them with generous pay, excellent accommodation and conditions aboard ship, pensions, modern welfare amenities'.

Wartime posters praised the vital work of merchant seafarers, but NEOU president Lord Winster warned in 1944 that he had little confidence in the promises that they would be rewarded in the post-war period.

The union had been a pivotal player in the IMMOA's development of the proposed International Seafarers' Charter and did much to promote its adoption. In late 1944 and early 1945 it staged a series of meetings around the UK, each attended by up to 800 officers, to harness support for the plans.

However, NEOU president Lord Winster told a Parliamentary debate in October 1944 that he had little confidence in the rosy future that had been pledged to merchant seafarers. 'They have heard similar promises and fair words before, and they have tramped the streets in misery after hearing them,' he pointed out.

His pessimism proved well founded. Within three weeks of VE Day the ship-owners put forward proposals to cut seafarers' pay by terminating the war risk money agreement. A series of emergency meetings was held by the Officers' Federation in ports such as Hull, Tyneside, Glasgow and Liverpool. All were described as 'filled to overflowing', with members expressing 'anger and disgust' at the 'ill-timed and ill-conceived' plans, and all resolving unanimously to oppose them until such time as a satisfactory agreement had been reached on post-war wages. Coombs told the 1946 NEOU AGM that the previous 13 months had seen more than 4,000 officers leaving the sea after deciding that present conditions and future prospects were inadequate, and it was therefore vital to fight for improvements. One member warned the meeting that almost 50 per cent of apprentices were failing to complete their course – many because they were 'badly disillusioned by the conditions they had to serve under'. The AGM voted in favour of a resolution on the issue, with members telling of the devastating impact on morale that had been generated by the owners' pay cut plans. 'When danger threatens and foemen nigh, God and our Navy is the cry. The foeman defeated, God is forgotten and the sailor slighted,' one member stated. In the face of the united union hostility to the plans, in May 1946 the owners put forward counter-proposals. These were deemed unacceptable by the unions, and it was agreed to defer discussion until the ILO's maritime conference had taken place in June.

The NEOU was active in producing and promoting the International Seafarers' Charter with the aim of delivering, in the post-war period, a 'fundamental and spectacular revision of the whole position of seafarers in the scheme of the world's life'.

Besides pay, NEOU members were voicing renewed concerns over officers' hours of duty and the need for action to address wages, working time, and leave for apprentices and cadets, in order to cut the excessive wastage rates. In 1946, in an attempt to tackle these and many other grievances, the union's council agreed to produce a British Seafarers' Charter and to work with the NUS to determine a common policy for negotiations with the shipowners. On 28 February 1947, following a total of 13 meetings, agreement was reached at the National Maritime Board on a package which set the highest wage rates in history, protecting seafarers' pay against the cuts originally sought by the owners at the end of the war, together with improved rates for apprentices and cadets, and increased leave.

The unions also secured an established service scheme which introduced two-year contracts – renewable for similar periods – for masters, officers and ratings willing to serve for such periods within the industry generally or with specific companies. The agreement also included provisions for payment during training courses, and for sickness and unemployment benefit over and above national insurance rates.

The 1949 NEOU general meeting began the battle for the recognition of electrical engineer officers, with discussions on a motion warning that in the interests of safety 'the introduction of certificates for competency for such officers is long overdue'.

This period also saw the NEOU resuming its fight for better conditions in the coastal sector, calling for the application of an eight-hour day, the provision of food and catering services, and payment for masters and officers undertaking pilotage duties. A series of intensive discussions with the owners resulted, in July 1948, in an agreement establishing a 56-hour week, the provision of a cook/steward on all ships, pilotage payments, and a reduction in the tonnage limit requiring ships to carry no fewer than two navigating officers.

The NEOU also worked with the MMSA and the NUS to press for an end to the long-running absence of any statutory manning scale for coastal vessels, producing in 1953 a survey of more than 1,000 British coasters, to demonstrate 'the inadequacy of the present arrangements'. At the same time, it was highlighting a progressive decline in the UK coastal fleet since the end of the war, with increased competition both from foreign operators and from road and rail freight. In 1955, in a far-seeing statement, the union argued that 'with the ever-growing congestion on the roads, efforts should be made to divert heavy slow-moving traffic to coastwise shipping'.

The wellbeing of members was similarly high on the agenda. In 1949 the annual report of the Officers' Federation outlined ways in which the lives of seafarers could be improved by giving them more home life, more time to make friends, and more opportunities for recreation. It argued that 'planes should relieve whole crews from stations abroad as crews are now moved from one part of the world to another to man vessels' and also called for assured regularity of leave, with adequate prior knowledge of leave arrangements on arrival in home waters, increased facilities for the entertaining of wives and friends on board vessels, provision of sports equipment ashore and afloat, and the appointment of specialist welfare officers. In the previous year, the NEOU AGM had debated a motion calling for married senior officers to be given the right to take their wives to sea with them for at least six months in each two-year contract; the motion argued that the impossibility of leading a proper married life was a primary cause of officers leaving the sea. Another resolution sought a national agreement providing for a minimum of 21 days of leave a year.

Although it had progressively improved members' conditions during the 1940s, the NEOU's 1950 annual meeting heard concerns of an 'acute' problem of officer retention, exacerbated by complaints that, as mentioned earlier, ratings could, through overtime, earn more than officers serving on the same ship. A motion calling for a 20 per cent pay rise for officers was put forward at the following year's general meeting, and subsequent negotiations with the owners resulted in substantial increases, ranging from £1 to £12 a month, and significant improvements in the hard-won agreement providing compensation for working Sundays at sea.

At the same time, the union was intensifying its calls for UK government action to combat unfair competition in the near-sea trades, making overtures to seafaring unions in countries bordering the North Sea and Baltic to raise their conditions to British levels, and urging the International Chamber of Shipping to establish global minimum rates.

The post-war period also saw the NEOU in the vanguard of moves to highlight the growing threat posed by flags of convenience. As early as 1947 its general secretary, Douglas Tennant, was warning members against working on Panama-flagged ships, stressing that on them 'you cannot claim health and unemployment rights or workmen's compensation.' In the following year he warned the union's general meeting that the time was approaching when some sort of blockade against Panamanian-registered vessels should be enforced. But by 1955 Panama, Liberia, Honduras and Costa Rica had managed to attract 9 million gross tons of shipping to their registries – a twelvefold increase from 1939. In the same period, the percentage of the world fleet owned in the UK had declined from 27 per cent to 18 per cent. 'The ability to undercut freights due to lower labour costs or to subsidies, and the spread of unfair competition, is a serious menace to British shipping and to the country,' the union warned in 1950.

NEOU national organiser Lawrence White was seconded to the ITF 'to take charge of the campaign which it is intended to wage against these sub-standard ships flying curious flags', and over the next decade the union was actively involved in the ITF's increasing efforts to tackle the threat they posed – including a four-day blockade, early in 1959, of the Panlibhonco[7] ships, which lacked satisfactory collective agreements covering the wages and conditions of their crews.

The 1954 NEOU AGM had seen the start of a campaign which continued to rage more than half a century later, with members voting in favour of a resolution calling for an internationally recognised seafarers' identity document to be established, 'having regard to the difficulties being experienced with immigration and security regulations in foreign countries'. In turn, this was taken forward by the union all the way to the ILO, where it formed the basis of a convention adopted at the 1958 maritime session. By this time, however, the NEOU was no more …

---

7 Panamanian, Liberian, Honduran and Costa Rican

11 Coming together: a single union for masters and officers

In his book *The Men of the Merchant Service*, first published in 1900, former seafarer turned writer Frank Bullen made a passionate plea for the 'several societies for the mutual help and defence of Mercantile Marine officers' to join forces. 'I will merely say,' he argued, 'that if all these societies would amalgamate, all pull together and enlist the sympathy and active support of shipmasters and officers, retired as well, they would be a body extremely powerful in their influence on behalf of the best interests of their profession.'

It took almost a century for his hopes to become reality.

The Officers' (Merchant Navy) Federation had been established with the aim of building a more united voice for shipmasters and officers in their national-level dealings with the shipowners through the Shipping Federation. In 1938 the recently elected president of the NEOU, Vice-Admiral Sir Edward Heaton-Ellis, warned of the damage being done by the continued existence of 'several organisations clamouring for membership and financial support of a Service comprising the relatively small number of, say, 25,000/30,000 Officers'. The creation of a single body to represent all officers was an inevitability, he argued, and would prove to be 'to the ultimate good of the industry'.

The anger sparked by the shipowners' controversial move to remove seafarers' war risk payments within 16 weeks of the defeat of Germany had brought the officers' organisations closer together. 'For the first time in the history of NMB negotiations on matters affecting shipmasters and officers, there is complete unanimity and singleness of policy and purpose among all the organisations concerned,' the NEOU noted.

In 1946 Captain Coombs sent a confidential paper about the future of the federation to the general secretaries of the MMSA, NEOU and ROU. In it, he wrote of the personal strain of juggling his federation duties with oversight of the NEOU and the IMMOA during the war, and he proposed a radical reorganisation of the federation and its operations. He argued that the federation should be the central propaganda voice for merchant seafarers – to raise not only public awareness but also to reach out to non-members in a quest towards 100 per cent representation. The paper also suggested a clear division of duties between the union and the federation, with the latter focusing its work on general legal and political matters, as well as technical considerations such as the revision of the Merchant Shipping Act, life-saving, regulatory requirements, and the Merchant Navy Training Board.

This restructuring was complemented by leadership changes. Following the MMSA's affiliation to the Officers' Federation in 1942, Coombs spent some time at sea serving as a staff captain with the aim of obtaining 'first-hand knowledge of current Merchant Navy practice and operation'. On his return he recommended to the NEOU Council that the time had come for a younger general secretary to be appointed – to reflect the younger age profile of the industry and to guard against the risk of the union becoming 'static or old fashioned'. As a consequence, Douglas Tennant was appointed general secretary of the union, and Coombs was elected as president of the federation in July 1943.

The cooperation agreement between the MMSA and the Officers' Federation meant that the MEA – which had repeatedly opposed the NEOU's applications for membership of the engineer officers' panel of the NMB – was now the only officers' organisation outside the federation. However, the immediate post-war period saw its relationship with the NEOU improving to such a level that during 1948 and 1949 detailed discussions about a possible merger took place, resulting in proposals to 'effect amalgamation on a fair and equitable basis'. Yet, although these had the strong support of the MEA general secretary, its general council rejected the plans in April 1949. However, in 1955, with the MEA facing financial difficulties, the terms of a merger were agreed, and a ballot of its members showed a substantial majority in favour of the plans. Welcoming the outcome, Douglas Tennant said it was a reflection of the way in which 'sectional representation has become outdated and ineffectual'. The merger, he added, would 'remove once and for all this stupid deck and engine room conflict which to some extent has plagued our industry for years'.

On 25 April in the following year the Merchant Navy & Airline Officers' Association (MNAOA) was established. The title was chosen after a ballot of members had shown 74.8 per cent in favour of being in an association rather than a union. The airline component, which the NEOU had been organising since shipping companies had started to establish aviation operations, was made up of around 500 flight navigators, engineers and pursers. The Radio Officers' Union had quickly established an airline section, and in 1942, following

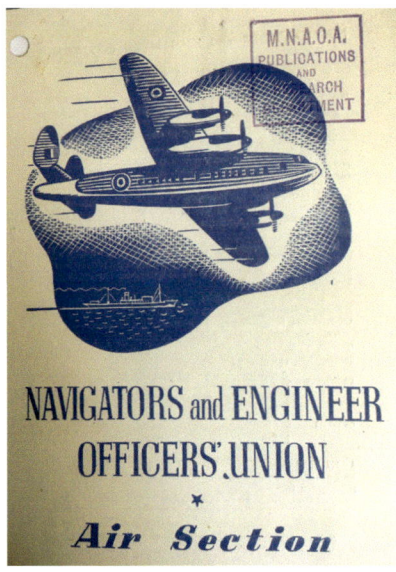

The aviation section of the NEOU, MNAOA and NUMAST was comprised of flight engineers, radio officers, navigators and pursers, and came to an end in 1990, when the remaining members were transferred to the pilots' union, BALPA.

negotiations with the NEOU, the British Airline Pilots' Association (BALPA), which had been formed in 1937, agreed to limit its membership to airline pilots.

The MNAOA inherited many of the long-standing aims and objectives of its predecessors, with particular concerns over the increasing impact of flags of convenience, unfair competition and technological change within the shipping industry. In 1958 the UN Convention on the High Seas had first set a requirement for a 'genuine link' between a ship and its flag state, and later in the year the MNAOA supported ITF efforts to secure an ILO recommendation defining the social aspects of this link. General Secretary Douglas Tennant, who chaired the ITF seafarers' section, and NUS leader Tom Yates were appointed to a special ITF committee organising a general boycott of Panlibhonco ships, and the MNAOA also helped to drive ITF efforts to follow up the implementation of the 1940s International Seafarers' Charter.

During this period the union devoted a lot of its efforts to dealing with other changes in the industry, including the increasing impact of automation, the safe use of radar, and the associated proposals for the revision of the collision prevention regulations. It responded to the rapid increase in the size of tankers by securing special pay rates, leave, and other conditions that reflected the intensity of work in the sector, and it also campaigned strongly for air conditioning to be made a statutory requirement on new ships.

Together with the NUS, the MNAOA was highlighting the damaging effect of high levels of seafarer wastage; in 1960 the annual turnover of UK officers was running at around 10 per cent. In 1961, no less than 38 per cent of apprentices failed to go on to sit their second mate's certificate, and the MNAOA conducted research which showed the impact of many new recruits being unsuited for seagoing careers, combined with an inability to cope with examination requirements, a lack of training facilities and poor treatment aboard ships.

A clear illustration of members' disquiet was shown at the union's 1961 General Meeting when 18 of the 61 resolutions called for increases in pay and 14 sought more leave. The union had sought to ease some of the recruitment and retention problems encountered by owners in the post-war period by arguing for the introduction of an eight-point plan that included not only improved pay but also greater financial recognition for those holding certificates of competency, plus improved compensation for working long hours and weekends, and more opportunities for wives to accompany masters and officers to sea.

Conveniently close to the London docks, Oceanair House was the Whitechapel head office of the MNAOA from the 1950s until the early 1980s, as the last of the docks were closed.

The MNAOA had inherited the long-standing ambition of raising the professional status of shipmasters and officers, and the 1963 General Meeting approved three resolutions calling for higher entry standards and the opportunity to train to degree-level standards through Ordinary National Diploma (OND) courses. The union had been involved in discussions over the creation of a new cadet training scheme for engineers, and had also met Ministry of Transport officials to pursue its calls for a certificate of competency to be introduced for electrical engineer officers, to reflect the rapid increases, in both quantity and sophistication, in the electrical and electronic equipment installed on ships. Also in 1963, the MNAOA produced proposals for an alternative training scheme for navigation officers, giving them the chance to obtain qualifications with national academic recognition and to progress to degree-level standards.

Early in 1966 the union was able to welcome the launch of a new maritime studies degree course at Cardiff University, which had been developed with its support. In 1970 it claimed further success with the introduction of new deck and engineer cadet training schemes, leading to nationally recognised OND and ONC qualifications, which had been developed from proposals put forward by the union following the 1963 GM.

The decline of UK coastal shipping remained a major concern, with the union tabling a motion at the 1961 TUC warning that the coastal fleet had halved since 1939 and that the 1953 Transport Act had helped to push freight from water onto roads and rail. The union worked with the MMSA, the ROU and the NUS to successfully lobby MPs over the unfair support given to land-based transport and to make the case for policies to provide 'a balanced, coordinated and planned transport system'.

Another resolution, put forward at the MNAOA's 1959 General Meeting, had resulted in the union launching a campaign for an inquiry into the carriage of dangerous cargoes following the death of 57 seafarers on board the British cargo ship *Seistan* as a result of a devastating explosion on board. General Secretary Douglas Tennant was subsequently appointed as the seafarers' representative on the government's advisory committee on the carriage of dangerous goods and explosives on ships.

Around this time the MNAOA had been actively involved in a series of working parties preparing the UK delegation for a major safety conference under the auspices of the new United Nations Intergovernmental Maritime Consultative Organization (later to become the International Maritime Organization). The union used this opportunity to further highlight its concerns over dangerous cargoes, and it also made important contributions on issues including the collision regulations and life-saving appliances.

The 1960s saw significant pressure for change in the British shipping industry, to keep pace with the broader social and political transformations. In 1967, for example, the MNAOA introduced the correspondents scheme (under which volunteer members served as a two-way communication channel between their shipmates and the union) which was somewhat similar to the honorary delegates programme introduced by the Radio Officers' Union in the 1920s. Then in 1968 the MMSA moved to improve its representational arrangements, with a rule change meaning that by the 1970s membership of its governing council went from being overwhelmingly retired members at the start of the decade to no less than 75 per cent seagoing members..

Wider social change was also reflected in shipboard changes, and notably the increasing presence of female seafarers. Historically, women's seagoing roles had often been confined to pursers, cooks and nurses. But the 1970s finally saw British shipping companies starting to recruit women deck officers and radio officers. To mark the considerable commitment of women members in one of the most male-dominated of all industries, and their resolution in overcoming frequent harassment and discrimination, the MNAOA Council agreed in 1979 to establish the Victoria Drummond Award, to 'commemorate the achievements and personal courage' of the union's first female certificated engineer member, who had died in December 1978. Named after her godmother, Queen Victoria,

Drummond had displayed a remarkable and dogged determination to serve at sea. Rising to the rank of chief engineer, she had been awarded an MBE and a Lloyd's War Medal for Bravery at Sea for her actions in helping to save the ship *Bonita* after it had been bombed in August 1940. The inaugural Victoria Drummond Award was presented in 1981 to Sheila Edmundson, the first woman member to obtain a Masters Foreign-Going Certificate, and subsequent awards have served to recognise a wide variety of achievements.

Pressure for fundamental reform of industrial relations within the UK shipping industry had followed from a 47-day strike staged by the NUS in 1966. Although the MNAOA had not directly supported the dispute it welcomed the outcome: increased public and political interest in the shipping industry – and two government inquiries. The first, chaired by Lord Pearson, examined the causes of the dispute, the terms and conditions of seafarers, and the relations between owners, officers and ratings. The resulting report noted that seafarers were working under legal provisions dating back to the 19th century, and proposed significant changes in the ways in which they were trained and employed. Pointing to problems of high turnover and wastage, it recommended improvements in personnel policies and fewer barriers between officers and ratings. The report helped pave the way for the sweeping reform of the Merchant Shipping Acts, to enable greater employment flexibility and less onerous disciplinary processes.

The NUS strike was also followed by a National Board for Prices and Incomes report on the pay and conditions of Merchant Navy officers. This examined whether a 10 per cent increase agreed by the NMB panels for shipmasters, navigating officers and engineering officers contravened government pay policy. It upheld the settlement, noting 'the need for officers' pay to bear a proper relationship to that of the men under their direction'. However, it also called for significant reform and simplification of the NMB procedures, pointing out that as the bulk of officers were now on company contracts their conditions of service should be in line with shore-based management. 'An officer,' the report concluded, 'should receive a reasonable salary and reasonable leave which takes into account the exigencies of service at sea; and at sea he should not be loaded with work beyond his capacity or denied reasonable rest and leisure except in emergencies.'

One of the strongest arguments for amalgamation of the officers' unions was delivered in May 1970, in the 250,000-word report of the government's Committee of Inquiry into Shipping. Chaired by Lord Rochdale, the inquiry had been established after the NUS strike in order to review the organisation's, efficiency and competitiveness, and the changing structure of the industry;

the report recommended radical changes in ship management, in seafarer recruitment and training, and in industrial relations.

The report argued that the existence of multiple seafarer unions was unhelpful at a time when job functions onboard were being transformed:

> Although we believe that the various unions representing sea-going officers have looked after the interests of their members well, we regard it as unsatisfactory that there is no authoritative body able to speak and negotiate on behalf of officers. While in the days of strict departmentalism onboard ship there may have been no great disadvantage in separate unions for different categories of officers, the situation is increasingly inappropriate today. [The committee concluded that] it would be in the best interests of all Merchant Navy officers for the MMSA, MNAOA and REOU to merge as soon as possible.

The MNAOA welcomed the recommendation, noting the 'obvious' benefits of creating a single union, and expressing a willingness to enter into merger discussions. However, the REOU executive said it was 'not at present in favour of a merger', and the MMSA Council declared that it 'did not consider in the present circumstances [that] British shipmasters should relinquish the specialised representational facilities provided through the MMSA'.

The report also recommended 'that every officer who is not a member of a union should consider his position, bearing in mind the value of a strong and healthy union, both to its members and the industry'. In fact, the officers' organisations had enviable membership density rates, with the MMSA having 95 per cent membership of seagoing shipmasters in 1955. MNAOA members were pushing for a closed shop, and a motion to that effect was remitted to the council at the 1967 GM before being agreed in 1969.

However, the Rochdale Committee concluded that a single union representing officers and ratings was 'an impractical proposition in the foreseeable future'. A motion urging the MNAOA to hold talks with the NUS about the creation of a union representing all seafarers had been rejected at the 1967 General Meeting.

Amalgamation was by no means unprecedented, however. Besides its merger with the IMSG in 1925, the MMSA had incorporated the Harbour & Dockmasters Association of the UK and the Mercantile Marine Trawlers Association in 1920, as well as the Sunderland British Shipmasters & Officers Protection Society in 1925. Following an approach from the secretary of the Grimsby Trawler Officers' Guild and subsequent discussions, the MNAOA took over its assets and membership

MNAOA members serving in the Lowestoft trawler fleet staged the longest strike in the union's history in 1980 – a three-and-a-half week stoppage, which secured a significant pay rise and recognition rights.

in 1977. Three years later masters and mates serving in the 65-strong Lowestoft trawler fleet staged the longest-ever strike by MNAOA members – a three-and-a-half week stoppage that resulted in the promise of recognition for the union, a rise in guaranteed sea pay for the officers, and an undertaking by the owners to discuss other outstanding matters in the future.

In the early 1960s the MNAOA made several approaches to the MMSA on the possibility of merging. It also held discussions with the REOU on the formation of a new union after the 1967 MNAOA Biennial General Meeting had backed a motion proposing a merger with the radio officers 'to the mutual benefit of all'. Six years on, the conference debated a further motion expressing disappointment over the lack of progress towards greater unity amongst the officers' organisations, and urging the Council to 'redouble its efforts to this end in the conviction that such amalgamations would be in the best interests of all officers'.

In the year after the Rochdale report, the MNAOA launched what it described as an 'expansionist' policy, opening membership up to shore-based shipping company staff. The strategy sought to strengthen the union as an organisation representing a broader base within the industry, and its success translated into an increase in shore-based members from 400 in 1973 to 707 in 1979. After the correspondent system (mentioned earlier), to improve communications between head office and seagoing members, had been introduced, further proposals to increase membership participation in the union were put forward in a report from the Tavistock Institute in 1978.

The MNAOA also took advantage of the continuing expansion of the North Sea offshore oil industry, in 1976 securing what was believed to be the first collective bargaining agreement (CBA) covering employment on oil rigs, as well as recognition by companies operating the rapidly increasing number of offshore support vessels.

By 1975 the UK merchant fleet had soared to an all-time high of 1,614 ships, totalling 50m dwt, and shipping companies were competing to attract British officers by making lavish promises relating to pay, leave and fringe benefits. However, behind the tonnage boom lay an influx of foreign operators flagging into the red ensign, so that by the end of 1981 more than half of UK-registered tonnage was beneficially owned by foreign companies. The MNAOA argued that this was threatening to turn the UK into a flag of convenience, with tax-dodging foreign operators taking advantage of investment grants and opportunities to use cheap labour, and with British officers' pay and conditions being among the lowest in Europe.

In line with the uneasy industrial relations of the time, MNAOA members showed signs of militancy, in August 1973 staging an official – and successful – 24-hour stoppage in support of the re-establishment of differentials on cross-Channel ferries. Then in 1974, after the government's pay board had moved to cut an NMB pay and conditions agreement worth as much as 18.5 per cent for officers, the resultant simmering discontent almost boiled over; the MNAOA and the Amalgamated Union of Engineering Workers threatened to call a progressive strike of MN officers. The dispute was averted by a change in government pay policy – but only three years later the MNAOA sent out voting forms in its first ever national ballot for industrial action in support of a pay increase worth at least £4 per week. This time, the strike action was averted only after the General Council of British Shipping offered productivity increases worth up to 15.5 per cent and 'phase two' increases worth between £2.50 and £4 a week. In a dispute in November 1978 members serving with the Orkney Islands Shipping Company staged a two-week strike in protest at pay differentials. The following period saw some significant increases in officers' pay, including a 1979 NMB agreement worth 19.5 per cent – and many members also benefited from the Inland Revenue's long-awaited introduction of income tax deductions for seafarers working overseas for a continuous period of 30 days or more.

Matching the extended reach of the British flag, and further boosted by a closed shop agreement concluded with the shipowners in December 1970 and formally agreed by the NMB in 1976, the membership of the MNAOA hit an all-time record of 43,758 in 1979. But the bubble was just about to burst: within the space of just two years the number of berths available on federated ships fell by 20 per cent, the number of officers seeking jobs through the Merchant Navy's Establishment Scheme almost trebled, and the annual cadet intake halved. British shipping was hit particularly hard by a global slump in shipping rates, triggering a surge of flagging out in order to cut costs. At the same time there was a marked reduction in the number of independent British shipping companies as consortia such as OCL, ACT, and Panocean Anco were formed to reap the benefits of economies of scale, and operators such as Ocean Transport & Trading, the Ellerman Group, P&O, Blue Star and British & Commonwealth increasingly diversified into non-shipping activities.

The MNAOA had continued to play an active role in ITF's campaign against flags of convenience, and had a leading role in the development of the concept of port state control. At the 1976 ILO maritime session General Secretary Eric Nevin headed the seafarers' side which agreed to extend inspections beyond hull and machinery – as initially adopted by IMCO, the UN agency that was to become the IMO – and into the realms of social matters, such as crews' living and working conditions. The union also pressed hard for the UK government to ratify ILO Convention 147, covering minimum standards on merchant ships, and to accept its subsequent participation in the Hague Agreement for a coordinated system of inspections by North Sea coastal states.

The drastic decline in the UK fleet and the associated job losses saw the MNAOA intensify campaigns to end the government's 'hands-off' approach to the shipping industry in the early 1980s.

The fleet decline continued to hit shocking levels, and in the space of just two months in 1981 more than 1,000 officers were made redundant, including 367 from BP Shipping, 192 at Bank Line, 165 at Furness Withy, 75 at Blue Star and 72 at British & Commonwealth. In 1981 and 1982, with the UK fleet losing an average of almost three ships a week, the MNAOA was forced to cut costs in response to the subsequent loss of almost 10,000 members over the same period, closing offices in Belfast, Cardiff, Grimsby, Hull, Southampton and South Shields, and shedding a number of staff and officials.

With many members struggling to keep their seagoing careers afloat, the MNAOA established an employment register for members seeking work, and in 1983 it turned this into a form of agency – Oceanair Services, later to become Seastaff International – which offered new employment opportunities, often on foreign-flagged ships. The union also went on to launch a personal pension plan scheme for the increasing number of members who found themselves serving with companies outside the MNOPF.

In 1982, when the Falklands War began, UK merchant tonnage had more than halved since 1975, and the number of British officers had fallen by around one-third over the same period. Less than a year before the conflict started the MNAOA had warned the government about the impact of the merchant fleet's decline upon the UK's ability to sustain itself through a protracted blockade, or to transport personnel and equipment. It had also warned ministers about the potentially detrimental impact of cuts to the Royal Fleet Auxiliary.

Admiral Sir John Fieldhouse, commander of the Falklands task force, said after the war that 'without the ships taken up from trade the operation could not have been undertaken', and that the vital role played by the 54 merchant ships during the conflict raised hopes that the government would finally recognise the need to protect and support the Merchant Navy from unfair foreign competition. Sadly, however, a lot of seafarers returned from the South Atlantic to be greeted with redundancy, as many ships in the task force fleet were sold or flagged out. Within three years the number of UK owned and registered ships had fallen by a further third. In response to the increasingly loud calls for action, ministers made mantra-like references to the free market, one of them calling for longer tours of duty for British seafarers and reduced manning levels on British ships in order to make them more competitive.

In the face of the continued threat to jobs and conditions, the MNAOA members became increasingly prepared to protest, and in June 1981 members serving with P&O's general cargo division took industrial action that forced the company to withdraw plans to sell four of its reefer ships and charter them back with foreign crews. This was the first time that the union had instigated industrial action on a company-wide basis in foreign ports by members on deep-sea ships. In November 1981 a sit-in by officers on two P&O Belfast–Liverpool ferries secured improved redundancy terms, and in January 1982 members serving with Sealink UK staged a six-day stoppage to protest at plans for cuts in services, leading to a freeze on redundancies and significant improvements in

MNAOA members serving with Sealink sailed up the Thames in 1982 to protest against cuts in the ferry services and the growing loss of British seafaring jobs.

consultation arrangements. In October of the same year, the MNAOA consulted members serving with BP over the possibility of strike action in protest at the company's plans to cut its fleet by 16 ships, with the proposed loss of 360 officers' jobs.

Things were to get even worse, however. The Thatcher government had a doggedly free-market approach to industries, the PM telling MPs in October 1986 that British seafarers had priced themselves out of work. Her arguments had been expounded by Norman Tebbit when he had addressed the MNAOA Council early in his tenure as shipping minister, claiming that measures to protect British shipping would 'shut out the most effective operators'. These arguments were amplified by the next shipping minister, Iain Sproat, when he complained in a speech to the MMSA's 1983 general meeting that British ships had higher manning levels than European competitors, and higher repatriation costs, overtime, paid leave, sick pay, study leave pay, bonuses and special payments. 'It is absolutely beyond dispute,' he told the conference, 'that the UK Merchant Navy has made itself uncompetitive by means of high manning levels and high crew costs by comparison with the best of our European rivals.' Hitting back at the 'siren, if sincere, pleas for more subsidies and protectionism', he went on to argue that these 'would lead, inexorably and not all that slowly to a more flabby and more cost-inefficient fleet'.

In the following year's Budget the chancellor of the exchequer dealt a further blow by ending the system of overseas tax allowances for seafarers and aircrew which had been introduced in 1978; it was worth between 5 per cent and 7.5 per cent of their income. He also removed the tax incentives for investment in new ships. Then, in a bid to make the UK flag more attractive to others, the government not only relaxed the long-standing officer nationality regulations but also sought to cut the regulatory costs of compliance with UK maritime standards.

During the 1970s talks over the possible amalgamation of the MMSA and MNAOA had proceeded slowly but surely, resulting in an agreement in 1978 to establish a joint management committee for most of their activities, and early in the following year a consensus on proposals for closer cooperation. Informal discussions between the MNAOA and the REOU had progressed to the point where they were formalised with the creation of a joint working group in 1977 to examine ways of achieving a closer working relationship. Announcing the move, MNAOA General Secretary Eric Nevin commented: 'It is no secret that it is my dream for an amalgamation of all the officers' unions.'

The discussions were not easy, as friction over the demarcation of the roles of radio officers and electrical engineers had soured relations – especially when the REOU filed a complaint against the MNAOA to the TUC over Shell's use of radio officers to maintain electronic equipment in the engine room. But by early 1980 the talks had progressed to the point where both unions agreed to draw up plans for a detailed constitution for a single organisation, noting that 'the changes constantly taking place within the industry indicate the need for members to present a completely united front to the employers to obtain maximum job protection and advancement'.

The rapid and dramatic downturn in the state of British shipping in the early 1980s, and the consequent contraction in membership numbers, had stimulated some concentrated discussions between all parties, and in May 1983 a special meeting of MMSA members was held to discuss the council's recommendation for a merger with the MNAOA. 'The current trends,' the MMSA reporter noted, 'indicated that there were compelling reasons why this should be so, despite a degree of reluctance which some Council members recognised as being inevitable and stemming from lifelong loyalties to the association.'

Once the MNAOA–MMSA merger timetable had been approved the REOU Council declared that it wanted to be part of the new union, and by February 1985 its members had voted in favour of a transfer. MNAOA members voted by a massive majority (8:1 in favour) to approve the proposals for merger with the MMSA and REOU, and the new union – the National Union of Marine, Aviation & Shipping Transport Officers (NUMAST) – came into effect in June 1985.

NUMAST was born against a difficult background. Commenting on the 'historic' inauguration of the new union, general secretary Eric Nevin wrote: 'Never have we needed unity more. Back in those days when we started talks, no one could have foreseen that a British government would have presided over the virtual dismemberment of the UK fleet.'

The fleet was most certainly continuing its freefall decline. By the end of 1986 there were just 430 UK owned and registered ships (of 500 gt and above) totalling 6.5m dwt, compared with 627 ships, almost 16m dwt, at the end of the previous year and 1,614 ships, almost 50m dwt, a decade earlier. UK seafarer numbers fell by a similarly shocking rate, the annual cadet intake dropping from a peak of 2,315 in 1975 to 1,274 in 1980 – and just 152 in 1983. Consequently, much of the union's negotiating work was spent in seeking to avert redundancies or to secure 'gross salary' agreements with companies flagging out, while members in companies such as Townsend Car Ferries and P&O's bulk shipping division took industrial action to defend their jobs and conditions. January 1985 saw three ships blocking berths in Portsmouth as a result of united action by P&O officers and ratings protesting against the company's plans to sell its Channel fleet to European Ferries, and in July of the same year, when Reardon Smith ceased trading, there was a sit-in by members serving that company to secure wages owed and severance pay. In the following year both NUMAST and NUS managed to head off plans for drastic cuts for members serving on North Sea support vessels, including a proposed reversion to the much hated two-on/two-off leave system, which had been put forward after a big fall in oil prices.

One of the most dramatic examples of flagging out came early in 1986 when BP Shipping moved its 29-strong deep-sea fleet to the Bermuda register. In a decision debated in Parliament following NUMAST protests, the company declared its 970 officers and 720 British ratings 'redundant', and stated that if they wanted further employment they would have to sign on with foreign crewing agencies.

This period also witnessed a slump in shipping safety standards, and was marked by some appalling accidents such as the loss of the British bulk carrier *Derbyshire*, the capsize of the ferry *Herald of Free Enterprise*, the Piper Alpha disaster and the *Bowbelle– Marchioness* collision. In all these cases NUMAST worked hard on behalf of the members and their families affected by the disasters, and went on to highlight underlying problems such as the ship design, ship operation, fatigue, safety management and unsuitable standby safety vessels which had been key factors in these incidents.

The union provided legal support for *Herald of Free Enterprise* members during the formal investigation, inquest and Court of Appeal hearings, and for three officers who were ultimately cleared of manslaughter charges during an Old Bailey hearing.

In May 1986 NUMAST challenged the government over its continued refusal to hold a formal investigation into the disappearance of the *Derbyshire*, questioning whether there had been an official attempt to cover up evidence of

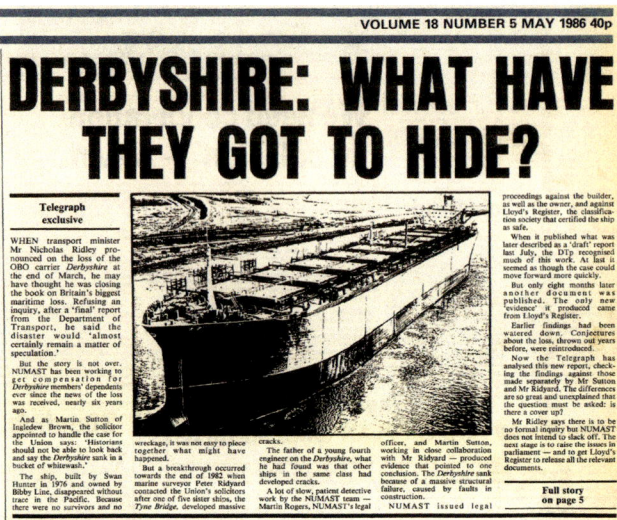

The MNAOA played a key part in the campaign to uncover the truth behind the loss of the bulk carrier Derbyshire *in 1980, challenging the UK government's initial claim that the causes would always remain a matter of speculation.*

problems with the design and construction of the vessel and its sister ships. The union also provided legal representation on behalf of its members on board the *Derbyshire* during the long-awaited 46-day formal investigation into the ship's loss. The union went on to work closely with the ITF during the successful side-scan sonar search for the wreck in 1994, spearheading subsequent calls for the formal inquiry to be re-opened.

NUMAST also took a leading role in seeking national and international action to protect seafarers during the 1984–1988 'tanker war' between Iran and Iraq, in which more than 540 ships were attacked and over 400 seafarers, including 12 British officers, were killed. Early in 1988 the union was part of an ITF delegation which met United Nations Secretary-General Javier Pérez de Cuéllar to call for a multinational task force to escort shipping in the area.

In this period technology was transforming the job roles of many NUMAST members. Following the introduction of the international Global Maritime Distress & Safety System (GMDSS) in 1988 radio officers were starting to disappear, while the number of aircraft using flight engineers declined remorselessly. Over time most aircraft had gradually dispensed with flight navigators and radio operators, and although the MNAOA and NUMAST had made a strong safety case for the retention of a three-person flight deck, the aviation industry was able to persuade regulators to permit two-pilot operations for new aircraft. In June 1990 the remaining NUMAST aviation members were transferred to BALPA, which had been providing back-up services to flight engineers for some years before then.

While the union had never taken a position of outright opposition[8] to GMDSS, it had sought improvements to the transition process, including more time to prove the reliability of the equipment and for officers to familiarise themselves with the system. It also fought against the crude cuts in crewing levels, arguing the case for appropriate electronic maintenance skills to be retained on board and for ROs to have the opportunity to retrain.

The 1980s had seen concerted attempts by the UK government to break up many of the traditional central bargaining forums for shore-based workers, and a growing number of shipping companies began to question the need for National Maritime Board annual negotiations. In 1981 it was the coastal shipping companies and ferry firms that were the first to float the idea of withdrawal from the NMB umbrella, and in 1985 UK offshore support vessel owners broke away from the General Council of British Shipping (GCBS) to set up their own organisation, just as the newly retired GCBS director general, Patrick Shovelton, lambasted 'all the rigmarole of the red book of the National Maritime Board'. In 1989 significant employers such as Cunard Line, Cunard Ellerman, Esso, Furness Withy, Mobil and Sealink pulled out from the national negotiating body. In March of the following year the British Shipping Federation gave notice of its decision to terminate all NMB agreements, including the established service scheme, with effect from 30 September, and to withdraw from central negotiations through the NMB from that date. NUMAST negotiated arrangements to safeguard members' terms and conditions, including the protection of past service entitlements, and it had to work hard to establish an effective system of company-level bargaining with more than 120 different employers as well as participating in the surviving national industry committees to deal with matters such as training, welfare, health and safety, pensions and warlike-area operations.

While the deep-sea sector had borne the brunt of the cuts, jobs and working conditions, the ferry industry came under increasing pressure after the plans for a Channel tunnel – which had been kicking around for over a century – finally reached fruition in 1986. When Sealink had been privatised in 1984 NUMAST had, by carrying out extensive research, managed to head off some earlier attempts to introduce detrimental changes in the sector, demonstrating the dangers of excessive working hours and successful negotiations to safeguard jobs, working conditions and routes.

The union joined a broad shipping industry alliance that lobbied Parliament about the threat that the tunnel posed to ferry services, but as construction of

---

8   The position was complex; as the technology was in place and the systems worked, the union did not resist the introduction of GMDSS *per se*. What mattered was the way in which it was being introduced, generating lots of extra work for masters and deck officers, especially in the early days as a consequence of the large number of false alarms.

the fixed link got under way, the operators wasted no time in seeking to slash their costs. In 1988, for example, P&O put forward controversial plans to cut its Dover wage bill by some £6 million, leading to a major dispute with the NUS which had long-lasting effects upon the industry. Following protracted negotiations with the company, NUMAST was able to minimise the number of proposed officer job losses, and head off the threat of significant changes to officers' terms and conditions – including live-aboard work patterns. But after NUMAST members voted by a voted by 4:1 majority to strike if management attempted to introduce replacement or foreign crews to break the NUS dispute, P&O threatened to sack any masters or officers who refused to sail with crew brought in to replace the NUS ratings.

By 1988 the UK fleet had shrunk to just 386 ships, 5.4m dwt, and with further decline on the cards the NUMAST Council gave the go-ahead for discussions with the Transport Salaried Staffs Association on the potential for amalgamation. However, given the long tradition of non-party-political alignment by the officers' organisations, the TSSA's affiliation to the Labour Party was recognised as a significant obstacle, and in July 1989 the discussions were called off. The MNAOA had earlier taken part in some talks on developing 'common structures' with the Engineers & Managers' Association, building on a close working relationship between the two unions, but these discussions too failed to move beyond the preliminary stage. A number of MNAOA general meetings had heard calls from members for a merger with the NUS, to create a single union for British seafarers. However, the links, already only lukewarm, between the unions deteriorated during the 1988 national NUS dispute, and the ratings' union went on to merge with the National Union of Railwaymen to create the National Union of Rail, Maritime and Transport Workers (RMT) in 1990.

Towards the end of the 1980s, as the shipping industry made one of its routine recoveries and as the effects of almost a decade of negligible cadet recruitment began to bite, a shortage of UK officers – most notably second mates and junior engineer officers – became evident, prompting calls from the General Council of British Shipping for the UK to accept officers from any country which had ratified the 1978 Standards of Training, Certification and Watchkeeping for Seafarers (STCW) Convention.

NUMAST expressed strong opposition to the owners' proposals, and continued to warn ministers about the threat to the defence of the nation posed by the growing shortage of British ships and seafarers. In 1988 the union took part in a series of meetings with the shipowners and the Department of Transport, which finally secured some support from the government. This took the form of a scheme to provide financial assistance for employers towards the costs of training cadets to their first certificate of competency, and for officers to gain higher grade deck and engine certificates, including command endorsements. Up to £3.5 million in support was made available in the first year of the scheme, rising to £5 million in the second year; it had an immediate impact, with cadet numbers rising to 427 in 1989 and 500 in 1990.

In the 1988 Budget the government also bowed to pressure from the unions and the owners by restoring some of the special income tax concessions that had been taken away from seafarers in 1984.

But with no signs of an end to the UK fleet's decline, in 1990 the government commissioned a joint working party under the leadership of P&O Chairman Lord Sterling to investigate the causes of the industry's ills and to identify policy measures which could improve the competitive position of British shipping. NUMAST presented extensive evidence to the 14-week inquiry, and expressed its deep disappointment when the resulting 70-page report, despite its acknowledgement that British shipping was a 'vital national asset', failed to make any specific fiscal recommendations for government action to revitalise the industry. In tune with the times, the report called for more flexibility in the rules governing the nationality of officers on British ships, measures to 'speed up and simplify' the technical procedures governing the registration of ships in the UK, and targets to be set for seafarer recruitment and training, also for the government to 'pursue by all available means the liberalisation of cabotage and reductions in the level of support for shipping in member states'.

NUMAST argued that the long-awaited report had ducked the core issues lurking behind the decline of the UK fleet; with the UK-owned and registered fleet down to just 274 ships, 3.4m dwt, at the end of 1992 and the annual cadet intake dropping back to just 350, the union launched a 'Petition for the Fleet' campaign at the start of 1993, in an attempt to widen the pressure on ministers to adopt more effective policy measures. More than 300,000 people[9] signed the campaign postcards, which were delivered to Downing Street at the end of the year.

At a time when global seaborne trade was forecast to grow by 70 per cent in the coming

More than 300,000 people signed the MNAOA's Keep Our Merchant Navy petition, delivered to Downing Street in 1993.

---

9 This was, of course, before the days of online petitions, so the high number of signatories is more significant than might be the case in the 21st century.

decade and when other countries' fleets were expanding by as much as 27 per cent per year, NUMAST warned the government that the UK was missing out on international opportunities to regenerate its shipping industry; early in 1996 NUMAST embarked on a new campaign – Sea Sense – to take the case for action across the country. The launch of the campaign coincided with a move by P&O to flag out five container ships and so, given that by 1997 the fleet had shrunk to just 226 ships, 2.12m dwt, the need for government action was clearly now more acute than ever before. Ministers finally responded to the growing concern about cadet numbers by launching the Support for Maritime Training (SMarT) scheme in March 1997, making £7.2 million a year available 'in order to avert minimum manpower shortages both at sea and ashore'.

In May 1997, following a change of government general election and the appointment of former seafarer and NUS activist John Prescott as deputy prime minister, NUMAST intensified the Sea Sense campaign, working with the RMT and the Chamber of Shipping. It saw these collaborative efforts rewarded with the launch of an industry–government working group to examine ways of reversing the decline of the UK fleet and increasing the employment and training of seafarers. Unveiling the resultant report – *British Shipping: Charting a New Course* – Prescott said that it set out 'for the first time, a long-term and integrated strategy for Britain's shipping industry' with a set of proposals 'to break the historic pattern of decline'. The 50-page report contained 33 action points, including: support for the creation of a Dutch-style tonnage tax linked to employment and training; long-term commitment to adequate funding of the SMarT scheme; endorsement of the concept of training levies; and measures to combat discriminatory employment practices in the sector. NUMAST gave a warm welcome to the plans, General Secretary Brian Orrell stating: 'This is a significant package and with the links to training we really have got a tremendous opportunity to redevelop our merchant fleet.'

The *Charting a New Course* report wasn't the end of the matter, however; it took a lot more lobbying and an independent inquiry under the chairmanship of Lord Alexander to convince the Treasury of the merits of tonnage tax – but finally, on 1 January 2000, the tax came into effect. A unique element of the scheme was its requirement for minimum training obligations – something that NUMAST had agreed to be prioritised over a flag link – with participating owners being required to train one cadet for every fifteen officers in service, or pay a levy into a maritime training trust fund.

The change to supportive government policies generated an initial wave of optimism and shipowner promises to switch their ships back to the red ensign, including a pledge by P&O to flag in at least 50 ships and to double the number

NUMAST's Sea Sense campaign helped to secure the introduction of a package of policies intended to reboot British shipping, including the launch of the UK tonnage tax in 2000.

of its cadets. Then in August came an announcement from Maersk of plans to double its UK cadet numbers. By this time, Maersk had 49 ships totalling more than 1m gt under the red ensign, and the UK-flagged fleet had become the fastest-growing in Europe, expanding at a rate some five times greater than the average for that continent. In 2006 the UK government was able to boast that 'in the past five years, the commercial shipping fleet owned and managed in the UK has more than doubled in carrying capacity – and the UK-flagged fleet has more than quadrupled'.

However, only two years after the tonnage tax scheme had been introduced NUMAST was raising questions about its ability to safeguard employment; a London Guildhall University report had revealed a 15 per cent decline in the number of serving British seafarers over the previous three years, and warned that more than two-thirds of UK officers were now aged over 40. The study also showed that some 1,050 new cadets were needed each year just to maintain officer numbers at the current level. But in 2001 only 468 had begun training, and NUMAST expressed concern about the owners' failure to deliver on their commitments to increase cadet numbers by 25 per cent year on year. In 2005 the union welcomed a House of Commons Transport Committee report which both upheld its concerns and called for government and industry to develop an employment link to the scheme.

By 2007 the proportion of UK officers serving on tonnage tax ships had fallen from almost 70 per cent to less than 40 per cent – this, within the space of just five years – and the union made concerted calls for the government to end the unfair competition for jobs. The anomaly had been created by the government's Certificate of Equivalent Competency (CEC) programme, under which an increasing number of foreign officers were authorised to serve on UK-flagged ships. Noting that more than 7,000 CECs had been issued between 2001 and 2005 – over 3,100 in 2004 alone – NUMAST told ministers that the system, by creating a pool of cheaper labour, was actually facilitating the replacement of British officers by foreign nationals.

The union had worked through the Merchant Navy Training Board to develop a new training programme – the Foundation Degree Framework – for officer cadets, which sought to ensure that the shipping industry could attract the high-calibre young people it needed for the increasingly sophisticated tonnage. Launched at the end of 2005, the scheme was intended to recognise the value of MN qualifications within the higher education framework, and to increase opportunities for personal development.

Towards the end of the 1980s NUMAST had managed to arrest the decline in membership that had been triggered by the contraction of the UK fleet and the dramatic job losses of the previous decade. The union embarked on a proactive recruitment and retention campaign, and went on to seek new recognition agreements in greenfield areas of employment, subsequently bolstered in the late 1990s by the government's introduction of statutory recognition procedures. In June 2003 NUMAST held a joint seminar with the Chamber of Shipping, attended by more than 30 member companies, to discuss ways in which the 'partnership at work' concept could be applied to maritime industrial relations, and the union went on to secure partnership agreements with many major employers, including Maersk, BP Maritime Services, P&O Nedlloyd, Global Marine Systems and Everards.

NUMAST also became increasingly involved in the rapidly expanding superyacht industry, which had generated extensive demand for British seafarers, and Nautilus worked hard to further develop its representation and services in the sector. The union entered into a wide range of strategic partnerships with other organisations in the sector and also became increasingly active and successful in tackling problems encountered by superyacht crews, for example, securing unpaid wages for seafarers serving on the *Indian Empress*, abandoned in 2017.

As the offshore renewables industry generated further demand for maritime professionals in the first two decades of the 21st century, the union not only sought to recruit and organise members but also to lobby government over employment and safety standards in the sector.

During this period the union also broadened its representational structures, with new forums that provided a more effective platform for women, young maritime professionals and LGBT+ members to become engaged and to have their concerns and issues progressed collectively. The core aim of the women's

Left: The first meeting of the Nautilus women's forum, in November 2010, was one of a series of moves to widen involvement and representation within the union.

Right: Opened by the Princess Royal in April 2014, the Trinity House Hub took the residential and care facilities at Mariners' Park firmly into the 21st century.

forum was to ensure that female members could contribute to wider discussions on standards in the maritime industry, particularly as shipping and maritime was (and is still) heavily male-dominated. The forum successfully established a guide for seafarers on maternity and paternity rights and another on bullying and harassment at sea.

The young maritime professionals' group concentrated on the specific challenges facing young workers in the maritime profession, including issues such as qualifications, mental health, mentoring and 'sea to shore' transitions.

The 150th anniversary of the creation of the MMSA was celebrated in 2007, and the NUMAST Welfare Funds charity carried forward its founding principles with an ambitious and far-sighted development programme to enhance and expand the facilities provided for retired seafarers and their dependants at Mariners' Park. A key element of this work was the opening by the Princess Royal, in April 2014, of the Trinity House Hub – a £4.1 million residential and community complex incorporating apartments, a café, a spa, a gym and meeting rooms.

During the 1990s and into the first decade of the 21st century, the union took a leading role on the international stage, successfully pushing for measures to ensure fair treatment for seafarers following maritime accidents, and to provide a financial safety net for seafarers suffering from injuries at work or abandonment in foreign ports, then successively securing national, European and global guidelines to combat bullying and harassment in shipping. With many seafarers suffering from the denial of shore leave as a result of increased security following the 9/11 attacks in the United States, NUMAST led the seafarers' group at the ILO to call for improved international identity documentation for seafarers.

Over the same period the union also did much to highlight the threats posed by piracy – initially in Indonesia and the South China Sea and subsequently off Somalia and the west coast of Africa – by lobbying governments to provide proper protection for merchant shipping in high-risk areas.

The perennial problem of seafarer fatigue continued to loom large in this period, and NUMAST continued to seek more effective measures to control working time, reinforced its representations with the results of research showing the shocking reality of excessive hours on duty. The union had been extensively involved in the 1996 ILO maritime session which developed a new convention, No. 180, on hours of work and the crewing of ships, and it then successfully pressed for its ratification by the UK and other EU member states. Not only were the ILO requirements a significant improvement on those set by the IMO's STCW Convention, but also they were enforceable on all ships through the port state control system. Nautilus UK – as NUMAST was now known as part of the build-up to its imminent merger with its Dutch partner – went on to play a big part in the EU Project Horizon initiative, which provided pioneering scientific research into the risks of watchkeeper fatigue.

12 Going global: transition to a transboundary union

There had been a long-running and healthy relationship between the Dutch master mariners' and mates' unions and their UK counterparts. For example, in 1932 the Officers' Federation had sent a letter expressing its fullest sympathy to Dutch officers of the Centrale van Koopvaardij-Officers (CKO: Union of Merchant Navy Officers), who had declared a strike when the country's owners had proposed to cut their salaries to British levels or to a mean between British, Scandinavian and German rates. A federation representative met Dutch union leaders in Rotterdam and agreed to advise his members against joining Dutch ships that had been switched to the British flag, for strike-breaking purposes.

Then in 1937 Captain H.F. Owen, representing the Officers' (MN) Federation at an event to mark the silver jubilee of the Dutch union, 'returned to London greatly impressed by the strong and efficient organisation which the Dutch have built up'. In the same year, the British and Dutch unions agreed reciprocal arrangements to aid any members in difficulties in the ports of each respective nation.

Cooperation developed further after the Second World War, when proposals were developed for an Anglo-Dutch agreement covering the conditions of officers serving in the West Indies. The Officers' Federation had also worked closely with the Dutch union and its general secretary, Pieter de Vries, through their mutual involvement in the International Mercantile Marine Officers' Association (IMMOA) until it was formally wound up in 1964.

In 1961 the MNAOA appointed a full-time official – based in the Dutch union's

MNAOA general secretary Doug Tennant, left, and Dutch officers' union leader Peter de Vries at one of the last IMMOA meetings, held in November 1963.

headquarters – to visit British-registered ships visiting the rapidly expanding port of Rotterdam. Relations were cemented further by the need for transboundary talks on conditions for officers serving with international companies such as Shell and Atlantic Container Line (ACL). In 1971 in a prescient comment about the future, outgoing General Secretary Douglas Tennant noted how the development of such multinational shipping operations 'must inevitably lead to an important extension of industrial relations', necessitating negotiations and agreements with unions in other countries.

In the immediate post-war period the Officers' Federation had flourished, and by 1957 it had a membership that included marine pilots' associations in Aden and Gibraltar; the maritime unions of India and Pakistan; the Australian, Canadian and New Zealand Merchant Service guilds; the Straits Merchant Service Union (Singapore); and the China Coast Navigating & Engineer Officers' Guild. In the mid-1950s, the federation provided practical support to the unions in India and Pakistan during disputes with owners in both countries, and it also gave advice to officers in Burma who were trying to set up a union.

However, by the mid-1970s financial and administrative difficulties were becoming evident in the federation, and by the time of its 50th anniversary questions were being raised about its future, the commitment of non-UK members, and notably its role within the International Transport Workers' Federation (ITF). Although it was hoped that the Officers' Federation could serve as an umbrella body to prevent disputes between unions when owners flagged out or changed crewing arrangements, its representative council recommended in 1979 that it should be wound up. This decision was put into effect in March 1981. Reflecting on the decision, the MNAOA chairman (and Officers' Federation chairman), John Roberts, commented: 'I don't think we should be too disappointed by what we have decided today. What the Federation was set up to do was to coordinate the officers' unions, and I feel that they are pretty well coordinated now.'

The MNAOA had a close relationship with the Hong Kong MN Officers' Guild, and as the UK government had in 1974 outlined proposals to establish a Hong Kong shipping register, the union seconded an official to the guild for five months, to serve as its general secretary and treasurer. Hopes that this might lead to eventual amalgamation were to prove legally impossible, however, and in 1980 the MNAOA arranged for talks to be held under the auspices of the ITF to clarify 'spheres of influence' for recruitment and negotiating rights.

Similarly close working relationships were maintained with officers' associations in New Zealand and Australia, which were put to the test by changes in the crewing of container ships serving both countries during the 1970s and

1980s. During the 1990s, however, there were discussions between NUMAST and the NZ Merchant Service Guild over the possibility of formalising the relationship through a merger, but in 1996 the NUMAST Council decided that it was 'not appropriate to enter into any formal arrangements at this stage'.

The demise of many traditional British shipping companies during the 1960s and 1970s and the rise of multinational consortiums such as ACL saw the MNAOA entering increasingly complex industrial relations. In the case of ACL, it meant discussions with Dutch, Swedish and German unions on the conditions of service for members.

After the UK became a member state of the European Communities (EC)[10] in 1973, the MNAOA worked increasingly closely with other European unions to develop a more coherent approach to maritime policy. In 1977 this came to a head with an agreement of all EC seafarer unions to hold a strike in support of a claim for the upward harmonisation of wages, hours and working conditions, as well as an agreement to stop flag of convenience (FoC) ships entering Common Market ports.

The strike never took place, but the issues underlying the claim were important for the MNAOA, which argued that the wages in the British shipping industry were the lowest in Europe and that some other countries regarded the UK register as an FoC.

Speaking at the inaugural NUMAST general meeting in June 1985, Kees Roodenburg, the president of the Federatie van Werknemers in de Zeevaart (FWZ: the Dutch Seafarers' Federation) warned that the FoC momentum was growing, and argued that European unions should unite against the threat rather than competing against themselves: 'If we from the traditional maritime countries want to maintain a merchant marine, we shall have to fight for it.'

With an increasing proportion of members working under foreign flags following the decline of the British national fleet, NUMAST intensified its international activities, taking leading roles in the development of European Transport Workers' Federation (ETF) and ITF policies.

NUMAST led the seafarers' side in discussions which in 2000 resulted in the conclusion of what was described as the shipping industry's first international collective bargaining agreement. The deal between the ITF and the International Maritime Employers' Committee (IMEC)[11] covered 60,000 seafarers from 43 countries serving on some 18,000 ships, and was significant in its move away from using the able seaman (AB) rate as a mechanism for increasing wages to

---

10 At the time the European Communities consisted of three organisations: the European Atomic Energy Community (EAEC), the European Economic Community (EEC) and the European Coal and Steel Community (ECSC).
11 IMEC changed its name to the International Maritime Employers' Council in 2012.

a 'total crew cost' model. It was also hoped that the move to improve seafarers' terms and conditions internationally through collective bargaining would reduce the damaging impact of unfair competition through 'lowest common denominator' employment costs.

The development of a globalised framework for negotiating seafarers' pay and conditions took a further step forward in November 2003 when NUMAST general secretary Brian Orrell, in his role as chairman of the ITF seafarers' section, signed an agreement with the Joint Negotiating Group (JNG) representing global shipowners and managers to create the International Bargaining Forum (IBF) as a cross-boundary mechanism covering more than 2,300 ships in the world fleet.

The union was also extensively involved in a high-level ILO working group which in 2002 produced a blueprint for a Bill of Rights for seafarers, which was to become the Maritime Labour Convention (MLC) of 2006. The initiative was launched after the ILO's 2001 Joint Maritime Commission meeting had listened to concerns over the low level of ratification of more than 30 of its crucial conventions governing seafarers' living and working conditions.

NUMAST actively supported the move to undertake a 'root and branch' review of the ILO's regulatory regime, noting that global rules were highly relevant to the more than 50 per cent of its members working under foreign flags. The union led the seafarers' side in discussions to develop the draft convention and to ensure that it provided a 'workable, enforceable and realistic regulatory framework for global standards applicable to the entire industry'.

NUMAST also spearheaded the employees' side in difficult discussions over international guidelines on the provision of financial security for seafarers in the event of death, personal injury or abandonment, and it fought hard to

NUMAST general secretary Brian Orrell, centre, deputy general secretary Peter McEwen, left, and Council chairman John Epsom at the end of the historic ILO conference in February 2006 which agreed the terms of the Maritime Labour Convention.

NUMAST spearheaded the creation of the International Officers' Forum in 2003, which aimed to improve the representation of maritime professionals within the ITF.

overcome shipowners' opposition to the development of mechanisms to ensure compliance with, and enforcement of, the MLC.

The significance of the MLC is immense, and it can be seen as the ultimate product of almost a century of work by the predecessors of Nautilus and other unions in seeking ways to combat the unfair competition and exploitation arising from a globalised labour market, with roots in the aspirations set out in the early International Seafarers' Code and 'Seafarers' Charter' plans for harmonised pay and conditions.

The hard-fought agreement on the terms of the MLC was not the end of the union's work, however; in the following years it was busy lobbying for the ratification of the convention and its subsequent enforcement. It also produced a detailed guide for members, to ensure that they would be fully aware of the 'Bill of Rights' that it had set down for them.

In 2003 NUMAST took the lead in launching the International Officers' Forum (IOF) – a grouping of ITF affiliated unions representing officers – and had talks with the ITF about ways in which this forum could be brought within the formal structures of the seafarers' section to enhance the representation of officers within the ITF.

These activities had intensified NUMAST's links with other unions around the world, and 2001 saw a series of meetings with the FWZ to examine ways to jointly work on behalf of members serving with companies employing both British and Dutch seafarers, as well as deepening existing cooperation within such forums as the ETF, ITF, ILO and IMO.

The first outcome, announced in December 2001, was a memorandum of agreement between the two unions, outlining ways in which industrial cooperation in 'Anglo-Dutch' companies could be enhanced. This was followed by a series of meetings in 2002 to discuss ways in which the two unions could cooperate more strategically and more effectively. This resulted in a cooperation agreement in November 2002 that detailed ways of working closely together on behalf of members serving with such companies as Holland-America Line (HAL), P&O Nedlloyd, P&O North Sea Ferries, Stena Line and Norfolkline.[12] Over the next two years this developed into formally coordinated negotiations on behalf of members serving with these firms.

In an announcement detailing the cooperation agreement, the two unions had noted that 'the development of a European industrial relations structure within the European Union will require trade unions to develop deeper relationships with unions of similar outlook and structure across national boundaries'. Such moves, they added, were essential in making an effective response to shipping's deregulated global labour market and the deepening crisis over the availability of West European officers and ratings. Both unions said they shared the vision 'that the future is in the specialised seafarer trade unions banding together to ensure that they are best placed to fight the challenges of the emerging European industrial relations scene'.

Building on the successful delivery of the agreed strategies, senior officials from NUMAST and the FWZ developed proposals to 'create a more effective organisation, united in defence of the interests of its members in a global industry within a global labour market'. A joint working group was established to examine ways in which the traditionally close relationship could be taken to a deeper level, with common policies, harmonised benefits and services, and coordinated industrial activities. In March 2004 NUMAST Council members held a meeting in Rotterdam as part of the process of developing more formal connections.

In July 2005 the process moved to the next level with the launch of the Nautilus Federation, a 'European partnership' to represent and promote the interests of British and Dutch maritime professionals, coordinating the input of NUMAST and FWZ into regional and international bodies such as the IMO, ILO, ITF and ETF. Announcing details of the plans to move towards a merger within the next

A joint meeting of the NUMAST and FWZ governing bodies in Rotterdam in March 2004 agreed significant steps towards the eventual merger of the two unions.

12 Now DFDS

three years, NUMAST general secretary Brian Orrell commented: 'When more and more of the legislation that affects our members comes from Brussels, not Westminster, building alliances with counterparts within Europe is not just a pioneering approach but also one that is essential to respond to the trends of multinational companies and multinational workforces.'

In October 2006 NUMAST became Nautilus UK and FWZ became Nautilus NL, as part of the roadmap towards a combined union. Starting in mid-2007, the UK and NL sections carried out a programme of extensive consultations with their members about the proposed merger. A ballot of UK members saw 83 per cent in favour of the plans, while a special meeting of NL members saw a unanimous vote in support.

The new union, Nautilus International, was launched at the 2009 Biennial General Meeting – 152 years after the creation of the MMSA. Announcing the 'momentous milestone', the union reaffirmed its commitment to remain an independent, campaigning and progressive organisation that speaks up for seafarers and protects maritime professionals whilst also matching the demands of an increasingly complex and globalised industry.

The significance of the new and special transboundary union was widely acknowledged both nationally and internationally. European TUC leader John Monks described Nautilus International as 'the first genuinely international trade union in the world', and predicted that it would be in the front line of struggles to combat the impact of the slump in the global economy. TUC general secretary Brendan Barber told the BGM that Nautilus demonstrated 'an effective union attuned to the realities of globalisation', and pointed out that 'when workers join together and organise across borders, they can be truly effective'.

ITF general secretary David Cockroft described the creation of Nautilus as historic: 'two of the strongest and most effective ITF seafarer unions coming together to create a unique union structure which crosses national borders'. But he also cautioned that the union would have a lot of challenges in the years to come, most notably with the fight against social dumping, in which maritime workers perforce accept pay and/or working and living conditions which are sub-standard compared to those specified by law or collective agreements in the relevant labour market within Europe.

Mark Dickinson, who took up his appointment as the first Nautilus International general secretary during the 2009 BGM, said he was immensely proud to have been unanimously elected to the post. The new union reflected the realities of modern-day shipping, he pointed out, and would be bigger and better equipped to represent members in the globalised industry. Rather than being swallowed up by a bigger, general union, Nautilus International would retain its identity

Mark Dickinson, the first Nautilus International general secretary, together with deputy general secretary Marcel van den Broek following the launch of the new union in 2009.

as a specialist union for maritime professionals, with an enhanced ability to represent members at national, regional and international levels.

The learning from shared experiences and the increasingly close cooperation in the run-up to the merger had already delivered some significant results, Mark Dickinson asserted. With a bigger profile and better use of resources, Nautilus International had a more effective presence in industrial relations and in shaping debate at European and global level on issues such as safety, training and piracy.

Building on the success of this amalgamation, in 2011 the Nautilus Council adopted a strategic policy of progressing negotiations with other unions, with the aim of potential merger, close collaboration or enhanced partnership.

Through its Dutch branch, Nautilus International took a leading role in representing the crews of passenger and cargo vessels operating on Europe's inland waterways. Revitalised recruitment and organising activities in this sector led to increasingly close work with the Swiss general workers' union Unia, and in July 2011 it was agreed to transfer Unia's maritime activities – representing mainly those serving in the inland navigation sector, but also some seafarers on Swiss-owned and flagged merchant ships – to Nautilus International. 'This agreement is a hugely significant development,' Dickinson noted, 'because it increases our level of involvement in representing seafarers serving on European inland waterways, where we are already the largest inland navigation union in western Europe.' Many of the issues facing seafarers in the inland navigation sector were similar to those facing crews in the international shipping industry, he pointed out, including sub-standard pay, working hours, health and safety, training, social security, and living and working conditions.

In 2014, to further foster cross-border cooperation, the Nautilus Federation was re-launched with a new constitution that brought together more than 20 unions from such countries as Australia, New Zealand, the United States, Hong Kong, Singapore and Belgium to jointly tackle issues such as criminalisation and fatigue, and to provide mutual support for members involved in incidents around the world.

Over the next decade the Nautilus Federation would go from strength to strength, launching the Joint Assistance and Support Network (JASON) in 2016, followed by fair treatment guidelines for seafarers, indicating what could be expected in terms of support and assistance if involved in a maritime incident. Reports into the future of maritime careers, were released, along with an investigation into the criminalisation of maritime professionals.

In 2019 formal membership criteria were agreed and established, including the requirement for Nautilus Federation affiliates to be ITF affiliates.

The existing relationships between affiliates enabled the Nautilus Federation to continue to work together during the global coronavirus pandemic of 2020/21, during which time it shared information and best practice which ensured that it could develop timely and appropriate responses and demands to the global crew change crisis and seafarer vaccination campaigns.

In 2022 Nautilus Federation affiliates determined that they should formally establish themselves as a federation, to formalise the governance of the federation and the relationships between affiliates. Discussions placed the domicile in Switzerland, both as a historically neutral country and also as a place in which it is possible to make such undertakings smoothly, under Section 60 of the Swiss Civil Code to establish a Verein.[13]

At a meeting on 19 November 2022 in Zurich, the affiliates gathered to hold their Founders' Meeting and Initial Board Meeting.

---

13 A Swiss Verein, also known as a Swiss Association, is a legal entity comprising a number of organisations – usually charities and non-profits – that have agreed to work together in partnership while retaining their own identities. Vereins and LLPs between them constitute the two main partnership models worldwide.

13   Going Dutch: uniting seafarers in the Netherlands

With its rich maritime history, the Netherlands has always been a seafaring nation, and there has been a long tradition of collective support amongst the country's seafarers. This was exemplified by skippers' guilds, dating back to the 14th century, and their creation of mutual insurance 'boxes' to provide financial support in the event of death, injury, illness or the loss of a vessel. However, it is generally accepted that trade unionism was slower to develop in the Netherlands than in many other European nations, and it was not until the latter part of the 19th century that the labour movement really began to develop strongly.

As in the UK, the early organisations representing masters and officers had tended to focus their efforts on improving their members' professional status or on meeting welfare needs. By the end of the 18th century a number of seafarer schools had been established, and College Zeemanshoop, founded in 1822, still exists, providing regular support for nautical students. The Vereeniging van Werktuigkundigen ter Koopvaardij (Association of Merchant Marine Engineers) was formed in 1898 with ambitions to enhance the status of the profession and raise technical knowledge high on its agenda, but the appetite for trade unionism increased to match a growing demand for improvements to wages and employment conditions. In January 1913 this resulted in the formation of a new union, the Bond van Machinisten ter Koopvaardij (Association of Merchant Navy Machinists, later renamed the Association of Marine Engineers; it has now become the KNVTS, the Royal Dutch Society of Marine Engineers).

The first significant Dutch maritime union was the Algemene Nederlandse Zeemansbond (ANZB: General Dutch Sailors' Association), which was established in February 1900. The union waged a short but successful struggle to increase wages and reduce working hours, and two years after it was established the ANZB joined the National Labour Secretariat (NAS) a grouping of mainly anarcho-syndicalist unions. The ensuing political divisions (which were mirrored by a split between members in Amsterdam and Rotterdam) resulted in the creation in 1906 of the more mainstream (or 'modern') organisation, the Nederlandsch Verbond van Vakvereenigingen (NVV). This developed further with the formation in 1909 of the Nederlandsche Zeemans-Vereeniging (the Rotterdam Seamen's Association, known as Volharding, 'persistence'), which joined not only the NVV but also the International Transport Workers' Federation (ITF), which had been established in 1898.

Meanwhile, in February 1901 a group of 30 deck officers met in the Café De Pool in Amsterdam and established a new union – the Bond van Nederlandsche Stuurlieden ter Koopvaardij (the Association of Dutch Mates for Merchant Shipping). Five years later the organisation, changing its name to the Vereeniging van Nederlandsche Gezagvoerders en Stuurlieden ter Koopvaardij (Association of Dutch Captains and Mates in the Merchant Navy), opened its membership to shipmasters. In those early years the association was extremely active, working hard to increase collaboration between the different ranks and disciplines on board and seeking to influence the development of maritime training and education, as well as working conditions. It successfully lobbied for improvements in shipping safety and operated a form of employment agency for its members, run in association with some leading shipping companies.

In 1911 the more militant seamen and stokers staged a successful strike in support of demands for increased pay and improved working conditions. The action was also to have long-lasting significance for negotiating arrangements for Dutch seafarers, as it was followed in January 1912 by the first collective bargaining agreement, between the Rotterdam Shipping Association, Rotterdamsche Lloyd and Volharding.

Masters, deck and engineer officers, and stewards had distanced themselves from the strike, their sense of company loyalty outweighing some of their pressing grievances. In 1912 a standing committee was established in a bid to pursue some objectives on a joint basis, but it collapsed in the following year after engineers took exception to articles in the monthly magazine of the Mates' Association.

Such divisions were damaging for Dutch seafarers, accentuated both by their exemption from the provisions of the 1901 Accident Act for compensation for industrial injuries, and by their exclusion from the subsequent law to limit working hours. Only after the outbreak of the First World War did the Netherlands government move – and then only hesitantly – to meet the wishes of the seafarers with the introduction in 1915 of the somewhat ineffectual War Sea Accidents Act. In response, members of Volharding, angry about its failure to improve onboard conditions and safety, decided to strike for better protective

Thought to date from the First World War, this picture shows members of the Nederlandsche Zeemans Vereeniging Volharding (Dutch Seamen's Union Volharding) under a banner which reads: 'Wij wenschen den vrede!' ('We wish for peace!)

measures. The associations for masters and mates and for engineer officers also demanded talks with the government, refusing to sign on until improvements were made. Ministers managed to defuse the situation with promises for action that partly – but never fully – delivered on the unions' demands.

However, the dispute added strength to the mounting pressure for a collective agreement for deck and engineer officers, and this was finally agreed in 1919. Recognising the value of working together, the two officers' organisations together founded the Centrale van Koopvaardij-Officers (CKO) in 1922. Two years later the Radio Officers' Union (Vereeniging van Radiotelegrafisten ter Koopvaardij en bij de Luchtvaart, founded in 1918) also joined.

This evolving unity came just as the economic downturn both triggered job losses and set back the struggle to improve wages and working conditions. The wider Dutch labour movement rallied to fight back, and the CKO formed four departments – port workers, sailors, inland shipping and land transport – to strengthen collaboration and coordinate resistance. While the captains and officers maintained their individual organisations, their cooperation within the CKO federation gradually improved, and through this work important progress was made in tackling issues such as maritime education and safety at sea.

Although as the downturn deepened the seafarers' unions refused to sign an agreement to cut pay, individual members were forced to go to sea for lower wages, and the officers did not escape a 10 per cent reduction in their rates. Further anger was generated by the decision in 1919 to exclude seafarers from a decree limiting working hours.

Suffering from both the global slump and the unfavourable exchange rates caused by the Dutch decision not to devalue its currency, the national fleet was hit hard, and by the end of 1931 around a quarter of all ships were laid up. The owners put forward proposals for a 15 per cent wage cut, and after difficult negotiations with the unions a compromise reduction of 9 per cent was finally agreed. However, the ink on the new agreement was barely dry when the owners put forward new proposals for a 20 per cent cut. The demands provoked fierce opposition from seafarers, and the CKO and the Central Association of Transport Workers (Centrale Bond van Transportarbeiders, CBT) decided to join forces in the fight against the cuts, setting up a contact committee to look after the interests of all seafarers.

Meanwhile, two shipping companies replaced their Dutch crews with Chinese seafarers and the management of the Scheepvaart- en Steenkolen Maatschappij demanded a 20 per cent pay cut from the crew of the Noord Holland, warning that if they refused to accept the vessel would be flagged out to the UK register.

The Contact Committee sent an ultimatum to the employers' association, and when members' meetings of CKO and CBT determined that the owners' response was inadequate they decided on 30 August 1932 to take strike action. The decision was followed with great unity, and ships failed to sail. Only two companies – Rotterdamse Lloyd and Stoomvaart Maatschappij Nederland – were immune from the conflict.

Although some seafarers were dismissed, this did not deter others from joining the action, and the decision by officers to refuse to sail proved to be a major obstacle to the owners' attempts to bring in scab labour. Strong support was voiced by British, French, German and Scandinavian unions, with the International Association of Mercantile Marine Officers agreeing early in September to render any necessary assistance to their Dutch colleagues. The unity shown by the officers ultimately broke the resistance of the shipping companies, who finally recognised the Contact Committee as a negotiating partner. After two weeks of strike action, they withdrew the plans for a 20 per cent wage cut for seafarers in liner shipping and proposed separate discussions for the freight sector – which, when the government refused to provide any financial support, resulted in a 7.5 per cent pay reduction. It was also agreed that no action would be taken against any of the seafarers who had been on strike.

The compromise was accepted by a large majority of the officers' unions and, although some of the ratings' representatives described the deal as a sell-out and a betrayal, the agreement secured the support of the CKO and the CBT and took effect on 3 September.

Up to this point the development of the Dutch maritime unions had concentrated on companies from Amsterdam and Rotterdam – and now the new contact committee decided to turn its attention to the coastal operators based in Groningen. It took some time to gain the trust of seafarers in this sector, and the Groningen employers' association was highly resistant to overtures from the unions, but moves to develop organisation and communications on a local basis paid off; following a seven-week strike in 1939 the owners agreed to enter into a collective agreement.

The Netherlands entered the Second World War on 10 May in the following year following the German invasion. The majority of the Dutch merchant fleet was at sea, and now was unable to return home. As the Germans advanced on Rotterdam, the treasurer of the central union rushed to the head office to open a safe containing 80,000 guilders to enable unemployed members to be paid.

The exiled government called on all Dutch nationals outside occupied territory to oppose the Germans, and around 300 of the country's merchant ships were immediately deployed in the Allied war effort under the oversight of the British authorities. A further 250 Dutch vessels outside the European war zone remained under the control of companies which had quickly transferred their offices to overseas territories.

From 1942 all 17,000 Dutch merchant seafarers were subject to a compulsory sailing decree. During the conflict almost half of them served on ships that were lost as a result of enemy action, and more than 3,300 lost their lives. As in the UK, the wartime sacrifice and suffering of merchant seafarers was largely unappreciated, with Dutch veterans given poor compensation and recognition for their service. It took many years for this oversight to be acknowledged, recognition, at least, now given through memorials such as the annual event, on 4 May, at the Merchant Navy monument at De Boeg (The [ship's] Bow) in Rotterdam.

Following the war the unions restructured their operations, with the ratings coming into the central union under the banner of the Union of Sailors. Masters and officers remained separate within the CKO, but worked in close cooperation with the ratings' representatives through the Contact Committee. There was also a separate Association of Dutch Merchant Masters which had been established in 1943 by a group unhappy with the closer links with the ratings; it was excluded from the committee's dialogue with government and employers on behalf of the CKO and the CBT.

The unions worked quickly to tackle issues such as payments to members who had been disabled during their war service, as well as new agreements to cover pay and working conditions, and the creation of new 'social partner' organisations for the shipping industry. In 1954 a Merchant Navy pension fund was established, but the composition of the board created problems as the owners sought to involve the Captains' Association in its workings.

Meanwhile, in the post-war period the connections between the CKO and the Union of Sailors became increasingly strong as they jointly strived to improve things for their members. In 1947 CKO, changing into a unitary organisation, ended its federated status, in which it had operated as an umbrella organisation for different unions. The movement towards unity peaked in 1956, when CKV – a new section for the Seafarers of the Merchant Marine and Fisheries – was established within the NVV trade union. With CKO part of this grouping, it was a strong and effective voice for all 'salt water' seafarers,[14] and it was active on the global stage thanks to offices in Curaçao and Jakarta, as well as involvement with the International Transport Workers' Federation and its evolving campaign against flags of convenience.

However, some ships' officers considered that NVV was a bit too political for their liking and they wanted a more neutral organisation to represent their interests; they launched the Association of Dutch Merchant Marine Officers (VNKO). Whilst this rapidly attracted a substantial number of members, it failed to gain much influence because it did not participate in negotiations with employers and the government. Ultimately, both CKO and the VNKO came to accept that this division was not helpful to their members and in 1967, together with the newly established General Association of Seafarers (AVZ), they agreed to establish a new federation of employees in maritime transport – the FWZ, which we met at the start of Chapter 12.

CKO and VNKO now worked so well together that they merged in 1970 to create the Association of Captains and Officers for Merchant Shipping (VKO). However, efforts to strengthen the central transport union organisation through the amalgamation of the NVV, BKV and the FWZ in the mid-1970s resulted in the FWZ's withdrawal from the wider federation in the belief that it would be more effective as a small and specialist organisation.

Soon afterwards, ships' engineers led pressure for changes in the way they were represented, especially at a time when integrated operational management was transforming tradition onboard job functions.

The FWZ had to fight increasingly hard to protect its members' jobs as the rise of flags of convenience and low-cost crewing practices began to dominate the

---

14 Those whose work takes them to the open sea as against the Netherlands' extensive inland waterways.

shipping industry and decimate the Dutch deep-sea fleet. While it sought to take a partnership approach in its dealings with the owners, its members were called out in 1977 on a national strike that stopped ferry services to the UK for several days. In 1981 the union fought hard against the proposed merger of the two biggest Dutch shipping groups, Nedlloyd and KNSM, and another successful strike was staged in 1987, when the owners of small ships refused to include the post of cook on board every vessel.

FWZ took a leading role at this time in pushing for a proactive European maritime policy to

Dutch members on strike in 1987 in a successful protest against owners' moves to remove cooks from ships in the coastal trades. Their banner, 'Zonder kok varen wij niet!', means 'We do not sail without a cook!'

protect member state fleets against unfair foreign competition. Nationally, it was battling for measures to safeguard manning levels on Dutch ships, to provide more incentives for owners to keep their ships crewed by Dutch nationals, and to boost domestic maritime training. In 1989 these efforts paid off, with a government decision to allow owners to keep deductions from seafarers' wages – a concession that cut the cost of employing Dutch crews by around 35 per cent.

The FWZ also opposed pressure from the Dutch owners for the expansion of the 'unofficial' second register, that of the Netherlands Antilles, in 1991; at the time, Dutch owners already had more ships under foreign flags than on the national register. In the following year, following a report which warned that without additional support further flagging out was inevitable, the Dutch government came up with tax concessions to encourage the employment of national seafarers and to provide increased incentives for investment in new tonnage.

The radical changes in the structure and operation of Dutch shipping increasingly blurred many occupational boundaries, and by 1997 it was agreed that AVZ, the General Association of Seafarers and VKO, the Association of Captains and Officers for Merchant Shipping, should merge under the 'new' FWZ – finally creating a single, strong union for all Dutch seafarers.

Like NUMAST, FWZ had needed to wage a fierce battle to secure employment and training opportunities for its members during the years of decline in the 1970s and 1980s. But in 1996 the Netherlands pioneered the tonnage tax concept, allowing shipowners to benefit from a tax related to the size of their fleets rather than the size of their profits.

The scheme saw marked initial success. Between 1996 and 2003 the Dutch fleet grew from 557 ships to 810, employment grew by more than 50 per cent, and shipping revenue grew by some two-thirds. But during this period an increasing number of other countries –including the UK – copied the Dutch scheme, and 2003 saw the Netherlands' maritime recovery suffer its first setback since the policies had been introduced, with almost 30 ships leaving the Dutch flag and orders for new tonnage dropping to almost half the number of the 1999 peak.

In 2010 a government study showed that the Netherlands fleet had become less competitive than many other countries. The government had sought to encourage the employment of Dutch crews through 'fiscal facility' tax and social insurance concessions that cut their costs by around 40 per cent, but the FWZ warned that only 800 of the 5,000 new seafaring jobs had gone to Dutch nationals.

The government had introduced 'flexible' crewing rules in 1996, which allowed foreign-certificated officers to serve in all but the rank of master, and the regulations were diluted further in 2003, with dispensations for owners to operate with foreign masters. FWZ managed to secure a safeguard under which the appointment of foreign masters would have to be cleared by a commission, and a company seeking a dispensation would have to prove that they were unable to find Dutch or EU seafarers.

By this time barely half the 17,000 seafarers serving on Dutch-flagged ships were Dutch nationals and when the fleet expansion began to flatline the union needed to fight hard to prevent the replacement of Dutch nationals with cheaper crews. In the face of these changes, FWZ secured an agreement in 2003 which sought to protect the country's maritime skills base by requiring owners to provide places for cadets and guaranteed employment at the end of training or otherwise to make special contributions to a training fund for Dutch seafarers. Just over 400 Dutch cadets completed training in 2002, and it was hoped that the agreement would increase numbers to more than 530 in the following year.

However, 2005 saw the shock decision by the chemical carrier specialist Jo Tankers to replace Dutch and Norwegian officers with Filipino nationals to save some US$5.5 million a year. The cost-cutting measures meant the loss of 98 Dutch officers' jobs from the company's fleet of 33 tankers. FWZ urged the Dutch government to use its powers to block the replacement of EU officers with cheaper foreign labour on Dutch-flagged ships.

By 2005 the Dutch-registered fleet had had fallen to 768 ships, 5.1m gt, and FWZ intensified its calls for the government to improve the terms of the tonnage tax regime.

Although the number of officer graduates had remained fairly stable since the scheme had been introduced – averaging around 480 a year – the number of Dutch seafarers employed on Dutch-registered ships fell from 7,650 in 1996 to 4,858 in 2004. Over the same period the number of foreign seafarers employed in the Dutch fleet more than doubled – from 6,100 to 12,906 – and FWZ urged the government to consider other innovative ideas to encourage the increased use of Dutch nationals on board.

At the end of 2006 Nautilus NL, as it had then become, backed an ambitious plan to boost the number of Dutch shipmasters and officers by 60 per cent. Drawn up by the Dutch owners' association, KVNR, the proposals sought to deliver significant growth of the country's merchant fleet over the next decade by bringing state support into line with other EU countries.

Between 1996 and 2003 there had been a 50 per cent increase in the number of Dutch-flagged ships, but by 2006 the total had dropped below its 2001 level: just 747 ships at the end of the year. As a result, the Dutch government hired a firm to analyse the policies of the past decade, and Nautilus NL was among the industry players providing evidence to the analyst. The union had become increasingly concerned at figures showing an overall reduction of enrolment of students at Dutch nautical schools and wanted to see more done to encourage young people to take up seafaring careers.

Nautilus NL worked closely with the owners on the resulting seafarers' labour market taskforce (TAZ), which announced its much-anticipated recommendations on 22 May 2008. Three key benchmarks were set, with the aims of attracting new recruits, retaining serving seafarers and increasing job satisfaction, to establish internationally competitive and cost-effective employment, and to increase provisions for nautical education. Although the Ministry of Finance expressed interest in the proposals, it remained reluctant to accept any additional costs.

Pressure for action intensified in 2009 when Nautilus and the owners warned the government that the Dutch flag had slipped to seventh place in terms of European cost-effectiveness. Decisions by Jo Tankers and Dockwise to flag out were followed by a further blow in December 2009 when Maersk confirmed that no new Dutch officers would be taken on, and that cadets would not be given jobs as officers once they qualified. Maersk told the union that using Asian officers in place of European nationals would cut its costs by 30 to 80 per cent. The package of support measures sought by Nautilus and KVNR had aimed to reduce the cost of employing Dutch seafarers by around 40 per cent, with income tax concessions to match the support given in countries such as Germany and Belgium.

Nautilus officials and members on board the old pilot vessel Castor *during a protest in Rotterdam on 4 November 2016 over Dutch jobs and collective bargaining rights in the Boskalis dredging fleet.*

In 2006 Nautilus NL increased its representative strength, announcing that it was joining with the construction union FNV Bouw to set up FNV Waterbouw, a union of 1,750 members active in the dredging industry; of these 300 were members of Nautilus NL and the remainder of FNV Bouw. FNV Waterbouw was established as a one-stop-shop union facility for dredger personnel and maritime constructors, with a back office of the parent union and specialists of both Nautilus NL and FNV Bouw.

Following a decision to merge FNV Bouw with other major FNV unions in 2014, the FNV Waterbouw members of FNV Bouw voted in favour of a transfer to Nautilus NL in 2015.

14   Swiss role: water work in a landlocked nation

The concept of a landlocked nation having a merchant shipping fleet may seem strange to some, but Switzerland has long relied upon waterborne transport for its economic and strategic wellbeing, the Rhine serving as a vital supply route from important seaports.

Following the opening of the 'new' port of Basel in 1904, that reliance increased dramatically. It wasn't an easy start, however. The first vessel to arrive (the tug *Knipscheer IX*, towing the barge *Christine*) needed a week for its 300-tonne cargo of coal to be unloaded by hand. On its return voyage, carrying 250 tonnes of Swiss asphalt, the tow broke; the barge collided with a pontoon bridge near Basel and sank, with the loss of ship and cargo.

The expansion of river trade created lots of new jobs, and in 1908 the Basel-headquartered Verband der Handels- und Transportarbeiter (VHT: Commercial and Transport Workers' Association) began operations alongside various associations of carters, porters, coal workers, removal men and warehousemen. Within its first year the VHT boasted a membership of 1,167, organised into 12 sections, and soon added a section for wood and coal workers. There was some initial strife with the union for food, drink and tobacco workers, Lebens- und Genussmittelarbeiterverband (LGV) – in particular over employees of the Co-Op and the breweries – but in 1910 VHT secured a cooperation agreement with the German Transport Workers' Union (HTV).

May 1911 saw the union stage its first meeting of dockers. After rapidly securing a 100 per cent membership rate, in July of the same year VHT negotiated its first collective bargaining agreement when it, together with the Rheinhäfen AG (Rhine Port Company), established a minimum salary and a 56-hour week for members.

In 1915 the fifth VHT Congress voted by 21 to 8 to merge with LGV to form the Commerce, Transport & Food Workers' Association, Verband der Handels-,

Raising the flag on a Swiss merchant ship in the 1950s.

Transport- & Lebensmittelarbeiter der Schweiz (VHTL), made up of 968 VHT and 3,609 LGV members.

1919 saw the establishment of the Swiss Towage Cooperative, Schweizerische Schleppschiff-Genossenschaft, otherwise known as Schleppi. At that time tugs pulled strings of barges – up to eight, the length of the tow totalling anything up to 1.7 km. In 1924 VHTL secured its first CBA with Schleppi, setting a 48-hour week at SFr 1.30 an hour.

While the navigational aspects of the transboundary nature of the Rhine and the Danube had been recognised in the 19th century, the internationalisation of work on the Continent's rivers and canals after the First World War led to new cross-border challenges. In response to these developments the International Transport Workers' Federation established a Danube Co-Ordinating Committee, and in 1920 the International Labour Organization conference agreed a recommendation to limit working hours in the sector. In 1921 the Convention of Barcelona further developed the legal framework governing freedom of transit on international waterways and recognising the right of landlocked states to their own maritime flag.

The inland navigation trade did not escape the impact of the inter-war recession years, and in 1930 the boat crews faced proposals for big pay cuts. The boatmen were paid in part according to an agreement made by a German union, and until that point the VHTL had refrained from organising the crews, for 'technical reasons'. But because the Swiss Shipping Company (SSG) was not a member of the Rhine shipping employers' association, separate negotiations had to be undertaken with them in Basel and Kehl.[15] Although the union managed to stave off the cuts during sailing time, the weak level of organisation meant that its members still had to accept major cuts.

In 1944 VHTL's dock worker and boatman membership totalled 143. But then, at the start of the following year, almost all the 100 or so crews of the Swiss companies and those based in Basel joined the union under an agreement with unions in Strasbourg. VHTL had also agreed with the International Transport Workers' Federation that it should represent the boat crews, and in 1946 an international conference was held in Basel, attended by unions with interests in the sector from Switzerland, France, Belgium, the Netherlands and Germany. Much of the meeting was devoted to working conditions on the Rhine, and the conference adopted a package of demands covering issues including wages, work and rest hours, and manning scales, which went forward to discussions at the International Labour Organization (ILO).

Although by 1947 the VHTL dock worker and boatman membership had topped 400, the relatively low level of organisation was an obstacle to the struggle for improved working conditions. Nevertheless, an ITF conference in 1948 adopted a motion calling for a convention to cover Rhine boatmen, reflecting the transboundary nature of their work. This issue was highlighted when VHTL faced problems in the year that the French government demanded that French crew members be paid in French currency; the companies refused to enter into a CBA until the problems with France were solved.

The union fought hard to build on an ILO initiative to develop an agreement covering minimum standards of working conditions. While the Central Commission for the Navigation of the Rhine (CCNR) sought to limit the scope of any convention to social security rather than working conditions, a special tripartite ILO conference in 1949 dealt with a proposal for two conventions, covering both working standards and the coordination of social security. The resulting Rhine Boatmen (Social Security) Agreement, ratified by Belgium, France, West Germany, the Netherlands and Switzerland, came into force on 1 June 1953.

The conference also adopted an international agreement on working conditions for Rhine boatmen, which dealt with working conditions and contained many of the elements the ITF had proposed in 1946 – including manning, work and rest hours, overtime, and paid holidays.

In 1952 the VHTL established a Rhine Navigation Branch (Sektion Rheinschifffahrt) and in the following year it formed a Seafarers' Branch (Sektion Seeleute) in response to the expansion of the Swiss merchant fleet.

---

15 In Germany, across the Rhine from Strasbourg

The VHTL union's first office in Basel – a re-erected allotment shed in the docks! – which was used between 1952 and 1965.

The idea of setting up a Swiss register stretches back to the 19th century, when companies trading overseas wanted their cargoes to be carried under the national flag. There were also calls for Swiss ships to be used to transport emigrants in better conditions than the vessels typically used for the trade at the time. Then during the First World War supply problems served as a catalyst for some serious attempts to establish a Swiss merchant fleet to bring in much-needed cargoes of food and other goods.

The lessons of that conflict were not lost, and in the run-up to the Second World War the Swiss government developed plans for ways to maintain all the country's freight connections on land and water in the event of fresh hostilities. In 1919 the development of Rhine inland navigation trade and the port of Basel had seen the formation of the Swiss Shipping Company, and in 1921 the Barcelona League of Nations Conference had established the right for states without a maritime coastline to have their own ship registry. In April 1941 the Swiss Parliament adopted a maritime law which enabled the creation of the neutral Swiss flag and during the rest of the war a total of 14 Swiss-registered ships operated, including four vessels bought by the government and managed by the War Office (KTA) and three run by the Red Cross.

In the post-war period strategic considerations resulted in a decision by the federal government to provide financial support to modernise the Swiss fleet. VHTL National Secretary Werner Brunner was a member of an expert commission set up by the federal government to prepare the draft of a new law for sea shipping. The resulting 167-article maritime code, which came into effect on 1 January 1954, laid down strict conditions for ownership and registration of

Swiss ships, with 36 ships on the books by this time. The draft code raised the minimum wages to those of the ILO Seattle Convention, even though this had not been ratified by Switzerland.

Seafaring had never of course been a significant occupation in Switzerland, but during the Second World War a number of Rhine barge deckhands went to work on deep-sea vessels, and Swiss seafarer numbers were also boosted by a drive to use Swiss nationals as radio officers on all ships in the fleet. The post-war period was the peak time for Swiss seafaring, with as many as 600 to 700 working at sea in the mid-1960s after the federal government had agreed in 1953 to encourage Swiss shipping companies to boost training efforts. Although in 1968 VHTL's seafarer membership dropped to 400, in the same year 15 Swiss nationals qualified as officers and 13 received financial support for training.

A Swiss seafaring trainee demonstrates the art of rope splicing in 1960.

By the early 1980s, and just before one of the global shipping industry's seemingly regular downturns, the Swiss merchant fleet totalled 32 ships, and VHTL had more than 600 seafaring members. However, by the end of the decade less than 20 per cent of seafarers on Swiss ships were Swiss nationals, but VHTL managed to persuade the government to introduce measures – including subsidies – that arrested this decline and saw a flurry of flagging-in to the register.

The boom was to prove short-lived, however, as a result of the increasing adoption of low-cost crewing policies and the federal government's 1994 withdrawal of the subsidies, despite opposition from VHTL; by the time it passed its 75th anniversary there were no Swiss nationals employed in the Swiss fleet.

Despite this, the Nautilus Swiss branch continues to play an active role in supporting the country's shipping industry and the seafarers who serve under the Swiss flag. Over the years the union negotiated improvements to all aspects of pay and working conditions for seafarers in the Swiss merchant fleet, including working hours, holidays, travel allowances, sick pay, death and injury benefits, and bonus payments. All Swiss-registered vessels continue to be covered by Nautilus CBAs, with ITF minimum standards.

In the 1960s Rhine waterway traffic also boomed alongside Swiss shipping; in 1965 VHTL's boatman membership rose to more than 900. Early in 1959 the ITF had held a Rhine Conference in Duisburg following the termination of the 'regional agreement', to which the Swiss employers were not a party. VHTL was also unconcerned by exclusion from the agreement, as Swiss wages were higher and also because the Christian unions in the Netherlands and Belgium were signatories. The ITF unions drew up a list of their demands, while the VHTL went into its own negotiations with its own demands on sailing and working time, and the introduction of a guaranteed wage to be financed, in part, by overtime payments.

However, in 1960 the international Rhine agreement, originally concluded in 1950 under the auspices of the ILO, came into effect. This instrument, which had been revised in 1954 and again in 1963, was designed to harmonise working conditions on all boats navigating the Rhine, and had been signed by Switzerland, the Netherlands, France and Belgium before Germany finally added its support in 1964. VHTL was an active participant in discussions over further amendments, agreed by a special ILO tripartite conference in May 1963, to reflect technological advances and new provisions for work and rest time, annual paid holidays, and special allowances.

During this period VHTL was deeply involved in discussions over the introduction of 24-hour working following the development of radar and other navigational aids, as well as negotiating on the introduction of push-boat operations. During 1968 the union negotiated over reduced crew levels and agreed a 25 per cent increase in basic wages to compensate for lower manning levels.

In 1969 the ITF Inland Navigation section met in Utrecht and adopted an action programme seeking to address such issues as the coordination of salary and working conditions, training norms, manning requirements and accident prevention measures. In the same year, the union fed into ILO and Central Commission for Rhine Navigation discussions on the implementation of the revised agreement on the working conditions of Rhine boatmen, seeking wider governmental support for the measures.

During the 1960s and 1970s VHTL secured significant improvements to boatmen's pay and working conditions, negotiating extra pay and bonuses for such things as radar licences and pilotage; working with dusty cargoes like bauxite and kaolin; and weekend work, holidays and overtime rates.

During this period the influence of the European Community upon the inland navigation industry grew markedly, and it began to address such subjects as working conditions, freedom of movement

A VHTL union official meets members on board a Swiss merchant ship in the 1960s.

and professional standards. The ILO agreement concerning the social security of Rhine boatmen was revised in 1979 (and entered into force on 1 December 1983) to reflect the improvements which had been introduced by European Community regulations on migrant workers.

The implications of the European Community's increased involvement in inland navigation matters were significant for Switzerland, as a non-member. The impact of the development of the Rhine–Main–Danube Canal, connecting western and eastern Europe, also served as a big issue for VHTL in this period, and fed into extensive discussions within the ITF. The ITF Congress had recognised the inherent challenges in securing the ratification of revised agreement on the working conditions of Rhine boatmen in the absence of any agreement on control mechanisms, and was also looking at ways to uphold standards in the face of the potentially negative social impact of the Rhine–Main–Danube canal.

As well as seeking to tackle a range of health and safety issues such as fatigue and excessive onboard noise, much of the union's efforts during this period were directed at the enforcement of existing agreements that were designed to harmonise working conditions. It also lobbied hard for action to address the growing problems of flag of convenience vessels and the use of low-cost labour in the sector.

Together with the Dutch, Belgian, German and Luxembourg unions, VHTL put up a strong fight against pressure to cut crewing levels on Rhine vessels under a review started by CCNR in the early 1980s and not concluded until 1987. Around 1,000 jobs were threatened, and crew numbers were also being depleted as a result of new and larger barges coming into service. VHTL membership in the sector more than halved over a five-year period, as scrapping to reduce overcapacity on the Rhine led to redundancies and fewer entrants into the industry. The union sought to engage national and local government in developing a strategy for the industry, and developed proposals for support – but failed to secure the cooperation of the owners.

Further blows came with the effective closure of the boatmen's training school in Basel in 1997 and the sale of vessels by companies such as SRN and Silag. By 2001 the Rhine Shipping Association was down to just two members owning five ships. VHTL, meanwhile, was turning its

The wife of a Rhine boat skipper moors the vessel.

Nautilus officials (L–R) Peter McEwen, Nick Bramley, Mark Dickinson and Marcel van den Broek at the launch of the union's Swiss branch in Basel in July 2011.

attention to the growing river cruise industry; in the following year it signed three agreements covering the conditions of cruise boat crews.

In January 2005 VHTL merged with the union Unia, which had four sections, representing members in construction, the construction trades, industry and services. Rhine boatmen and Swiss seafarers were part of the transport and logistics element of the services section, and under the merger agreement the union office in Basel docks – which had been established in 1952 by former VHTL secretary Karl Rebsamen – was retained. The serving secretary, Nick Bramley, became a local secretary for transport and logistics, with responsibilities including river docks, and Rhine and deep-sea shipping, and he continued as ETF and ITF section chair.

The merger did not work out very well, however, and within 18 months Unia was forced to make deep cuts as a consequence of financial difficulties. Around 10 per cent of staff were made redundant, and in May 2006 the Basel docks office was closed. Around this time, contacts with Nautilus NL resulted in discussions about a transfer of the Swiss shipping and inland navigation activities, membership and secretariat to Nautilus International. Following a series of negotiations, the Unia Central Committee agreed in April 2011 to the transfer proposals, and after the founding on 7 June of a Swiss association (to comply with Swiss law) named Nautilus International, the new branch was formed on 1 July 2011 in Basel.

15 Strength in unification: a union fit for the future

Buoyed by the successful merger in 2009 and the subsequent expansion into Switzerland, Nautilus International continued to strengthen its global role through its work to develop the Nautilus Federation and the International Officers' Federation. At the launch meeting leaders of the new union set out clear strategic aims and objectives, with the need to rebuild the Dutch and British seafarer skills base at the top of the list. Shipping safety, fatigue and fair treatment were also priority policy issues, along with action to tackle the threat of piracy and to promote the successful adoption and enforcement of the MLC, urging governments not only to ratify the convention but also to actively implement its provisions.

All this was against the challenging background of a global economic crisis which had severely affected shipping markets. However, general secretary Mark Dickinson told the 2011 General Meeting that the creation of Nautilus International 'has given us an increased ability to confront such challenges and to take the lead in finding innovative and imaginative solutions.' With companies such as Maersk and Jo Tankers announcing significant redundancies, Nautilus sought to minimise the impact on members by ensuring that the vast majority of job losses were on a voluntary rather than compulsory basis, and it fought to defend members' terms and conditions from planned cuts.

This period was marked by a series of high-profile cases involving the prosecution and imprisonment of shipmasters and officers, many of them after incidents whose causes lay far outside the control of the accused. Not only did Nautilus organise the legal defence of members – such as helping to secure a not guilty verdict for a master prosecuted after three crew members had died in an enclosed space on his ship – but also it led efforts to secure global guidelines for the fair treatment of seafarers following maritime accidents.

Although the IMO and ILO had adopted the guidelines in 2006, the union was concerned that masters and officers were still continuing to be targeted as easy scapegoats following accidents. To combat the criminalisation of seafarers and to provide a practical response, the Nautilus Federation in 2016 launched the Joint Assistance and Support Network (JASON), supported by Nautilus 24/7 – a round- the-clock multilingual helpline run by the International Seafarers' Welfare and Assistance Network (ISWAN). Through JASON, the Nautilus Federation was able to offer mutual assistance and support for all seafarers belonging to federation unions.

Nautilus International continued to campaign to ensure that the IMO/ILO guidelines were fully observed when seafarers were interviewed by a law enforcement authority following an incident. It also proposed further improvements to the guidelines, following a survey in October 2019 which found that 90 per cent of seafarers questioned said they were concerned about criminalisation and two-thirds said it impacted the way they felt about working at sea.

In 2010 the union kicked off a successful campaign to tackle the dangers of asbestos on board ships following the discovery of a newly built Dutch chemical tanker which was 'riddled' with the deadly substance. Nautilus investigations revealed that this was by no means a unique case and that, despite the SOLAS (Safety of Life at Sea) Convention rules intended to restrict the use of asbestos on new ships, many shipyards around the world were continuing to use the substance in areas such as fire bulkheads, ceiling panels, exhaust and pipeline insulation, gaskets and electrical installations. The union took the case to the IMO, which subsequently urged flag states to prevent the future use of asbestos and to 'take appropriate action' in cases where the SOLAS rules were found to be flouted.

Nautilus also took a lead in developing programmes to combat bullying and harassment within the shipping industry. Following an initial survey of members which revealed the shocking scale of the problem, it worked in 2002 with British owners, then in 2004 with European owners, to develop guidelines to tackle it. In 2016 this work culminated with the publication by the ITF and the International Chamber of Shipping on global guidance to eliminate shipboard harassment and bullying.

The need for such action had been highlighted by Nautilus in 2010 when Akhona Geveza, a South African cadet serving on the British-registered ship *Safmarine Kariba*, died in mysterious circumstances soon after alleging that she had been raped by the Ukrainian chief officer. Nautilus not only pressed for a full inquiry into the case but also secured a debate in the House of Lords and questions in the House of Commons. The union's calls for shipowners to review their equal opportunities policies and to improve arrangements for seafarers to report problems on board their vessels resulted in a project to overhaul the 2004 European guidelines, including improved training materials and awareness-raising efforts.

Piracy has long been a problem in the shipping industry, but early in the 21st century the number of attacks, as well as their intensity, hit unprecedented levels. In 2010 alone, more than 4,100 seafarers were attacked and almost 1,100 held hostage. As the levels of violence and intimidation against seafarers spiralled, Nautilus was in the forefront of calls for more effective protection to be put in place. It helped to secure the deployment of multinational naval counter-piracy patrols in the Gulf of Aden and the Indian Ocean, and lobbied strongly for similar forces to be put in place off the coast of West Africa after a sustained spate of vicious attacks in the region. The union met the British and Dutch governments to discuss issues such as the use of armed guards on merchant ships, and also took part in national and international negotiations on warlike operations area agreements.

Nautilus had also been a key partner in the EU-funded Project Horizon, which concluded its work in 2012 with a report revealing that as many as 45 per cent of watchkeepers fell asleep on duty during six-on/six-off work patterns and up to 40 per cent on four/eight rotas. While pressing for more action to address the long-standing risks of fatigue, in the same year the union was successful in helping to negotiate a Europe-wide agreement to limit the working hours of crews on inland waterway vessels.

Further challenges came with the oil price collapse of 2015, which led to significant redundancies in the offshore oil and gas sector. Nautilus fought, with some success, to minimise the job losses, and also continued to develop its membership through new agreements in the offshore renewables sector, by introducing new services for members serving on superyachts and by seeking to recruit within Europe's rivercruise industry.

In 2016 the result of the UK's Brexit referendum presented a challenge to the principles upon which Nautilus International had been founded. The union's council had unanimously endorsed a 'remain' policy, on the basis that this was in the best interests of members and the industry in which they worked, and the union lobbied ministers for safeguards on issues such as the continued mutual recognition of certificates of competency.

In 2019 the union secured a major milestone in the rivercruise sector, signing the first ever collective bargaining agreement for members in a hitherto largely unregulated cross-border industry. The Switzerland branch was also kept busy in seeking not only to safeguard the future of the Swiss ship register, but also to prevent it from becoming another flag of convenience.

Consolidating its many years of hard work to help develop the MLC, Nautilus was in the forefront of further efforts to take it forward as a 'living' convention. In 2014 input from the union was highly influential in securing amendments addressing such issues as abandoned seafarers, bullying and harassment, and protection for crew members held hostage on their ships. Further amendments were agreed in 2022, including the need for seafarers to have internet access, and to have appropriately sized personal protective equipment; for good-quality drinking water to be available free of charge; and for states to ensure the prompt repatriation of abandoned seafarers and to provide medical care for seafarers in need of immediate assistance.

In 2018 Nautilus secured an important employment tribunal ruling in its long-running efforts to uphold the employment rights of British seafarers. The judgment upheld the union's arguments that members serving with Seahorse Maritime were entitled to collective consultation ahead of a large redundancy exercise, as they had 'a sufficiently strong connection to Great Britain', and when travelling between the UK and their ships were 'on company business'. Although the Court of Appeal then backed the company's appeal against the ruling, Nautilus eventually secured a judgment that members were entitled to individual statutory redundancy payments, and more than £223,000 was paid in compensation to those involved in the claims.

During the austerity cuts in UK public spending from 2010, Nautilus had worked hard to develop a united industry defence of the existing measures to support shipping and seafarer employment – especially in summer 2011, in the face of a review of the SMarT training assistance scheme. But fresh hopes of a revival in the fortunes of the British merchant fleet were raised in September 2015, when the UK government published its Maritime Growth Study – the result of an extensive programme of industry-wide consultations launched in response to continuing concerns about the contraction of the UK shipping industry. The 137-page report set out 18 recommendations seeking to maintain the UK's position as a world-leading maritime centre, including a call to develop a skills strategy to safeguard the supply of UK seafarers. Though disappointed by the way in which the report appeared to have 'kicked the difficult decisions into the long grass', Nautilus welcomed the fact that 9 of its 18 recommendations covered employment and training, and the union pledged support for its proposals to develop 'a skills strategy with focused objectives for addressing these concerns'.

However, Nautilus, becoming increasingly disturbed by the slow progress on the report's recommendations, also continued to express disquiet about the lack of any substantive action to ensure that cadet numbers would come anywhere near the level needed to meet future needs. As a result the union then worked closely with the UK Chamber of Shipping to develop proposals for a SMarT Plus package of measures, to ensure that UK support for training kept pace with that of other countries. Nautilus was successful in securing the government's agreement early in 2018 to double the budget for the scheme – a move which, it was hoped, would raise the annual cadet intake from around 750 to more than 1,200.

In 2017 the government began to talk confidently about doubling the size of the UK fleet, and early in the following year more optimism was generated when it launched another new initiative – Maritime 2050 – which promised to build on the Maritime Growth Study by taking a 'once in a generation opportunity' to develop a long-term policy platform for the sector. Nautilus made a detailed submission to a consultation on the plans, which had the by now familiar aims of identifying ways to keep the UK as a global leader in key maritime sectors, calling for: improved assistance for training and employment; improvements to the tonnage tax scheme; and measures to encourage UK-owned ships to use the UK flag. The union welcomed the proposals set out in the subsequent Maritime 2050 policy paper, published in February 2019, although it expressed concern at the absence, once again, of defined targets for fleet growth and job creation.

Highlighting cases of exploitation on board vessels running in and out of British ports, Nautilus intensified its campaign to have the National Minimum Wage (NMW) rules extended to all seafarers working in UK waters. This helped to persuade ministers to establish a working group in 2017 to assess the legal issues, and in May 2020 the government finally introduced regulations extending the provisions of the NMW to all seafarers in UK territorial waters, including one-port voyages on the UK continental shelf. In the following month Nautilus' lobbying over the 'social dumping' of low-cost crews in British waters paid off, with the government's agreement to apply a post-Brexit points-based immigration system to the issuance of working visas to foreign seafarers.

In June 2020 Nautilus joined the newly formed Maritime Skills Commission, which had been set up by the government to: investigate the existing and future skills needs of the industry both on land and at sea; attract more people to the sector; ensure career progression; and futureproof training for employees.

However, the concerted efforts to establish a better future for the British shipping industry and its seafarers were soon to be shockingly undermined …

16 'A day that will live in infamy': P&O Ferries undermines recovery plans

At 7.27 in the morning of 17 March 2022 P&O Ferries kicked off what Nautilus general secretary Mark Dickinson described as 'a day that will live in infamy in the history of the British maritime industry'.

A tweet from the company announced that 'services are unable to run for the next few days. We are advising travellers of alternative arrangements'. Its ships at sea were told to return to port and discharge their passengers and vehicles, and the entire eight-vessel fleet was instructed to remain alongside to await further instructions.

Rumours began to spread that coaches with security guards had arrived in ports; early reports of an imminent 'major announcement' by the company were found to be correct, in that it materialised at 11.00 a.m. It was the ruthless – and illegal – dismissal of the company's 786 seafarers with no notice or consultation. Its seafaring staff were informed by a pre-recorded three-minute video message from management that their contracts were being severed with immediate effect, and that they would be replaced with cheaper crews employed through the Glasgow-based Clyde Marine Recruitment and a Maltese agency, International Ferry Management.

P&O Ferries claimed it had clocked up an unsustainable year-on-year loss of £100 million, and that it would not survive without 'making swift and significant changes now'. In a letter to employees, CEO Peter Hebblethwaite explained that the move would halve the company's crewing costs and would 'enable us to better compete and be more responsive to our customers' needs'.

Over the next couple of hours, in scenes that one Nautilus member described as 'like a military operation', seafarers were forced off their ships by security guards – often with just a few minutes' notice to leave their vessel. One long-serving seafarer said that although he had been working nights he was woken in his cabin at 11 a.m. and told to leave the ship immediately. Others were given two hours in which to retrieve all their belongings, and were escorted by security staff as they collected their effects. Outrage over these 'callous' actions intensified when Nautilus was subsequently given a photograph showing some personal effects lying next to a rubbish skip on one ship.

P&O Ferries gave the seafarers a two-week ultimatum to accept or forfeit an 'enhanced severance package', totalling some £36.5 million, to reflect the breach of their employment rights. The offer included a non-disclosure agreement, prohibiting crew from discussing P&O Ferries and from taking further legal action.

The company's actions were widely condemned, attracting intense media scrutiny and heated political debate. The TUC described the sackings as 'a national scandal', and said it should serve as 'a turning point for workers' rights'. Prime Minister Boris Johnson's office said the way in which the redundancies had been made was 'completely unacceptable', and maritime minister Robert Courts said he was 'extremely concerned and frankly angry at the treatment' of the crews.

For Nautilus the move represented the consequence of its long-standing but unheeded warnings about 'glaring gaps' in employment protection for British seafarers and the abysmal failure by government to reverse the 'race to the bottom' in the shipping industry – even within the country's own waters. For well over a decade before the P&O Ferries sackings, Nautilus had been pressing for action to prevent the ferry sector – described as one of the last bastions of British seafarer employment – from suffering the cut-price crewing practices that had spread throughout the deep-sea fleets. Nautilus had worked with other unions in the UK, the Netherlands and Switzerland, and indeed across Europe, to highlight the many detrimental effects arising from the use of low-cost foreign crews and the need for action to create a level playing field for terms and conditions. The union had also made progress in a long-running lobby of ministers for measures to extend the UK NMW to all seafarers working in the UK's waters.

But in the previous year, in June 2021, the rising tide of competitive pressure had washed into Dover when Irish Ferries began operating to Calais with the Cyprus-flagged *Isle of Inishmore* after P&O Ferries had withdrawn two ships from the route. In an uncanny parallel of P&O Ferries' actions, Irish Ferries had triggered a bitter three-week dispute in 2005 when it had moved to replace more than 540 British and Irish seafarers with cheaper, eastern European, agency crews. Its resulting crewing model – condemned by the unions – meant that some of its seafarers were paid below NMW rates and worked much longer hours and tours of duty than those serving with other operators.

In the immediate aftermath of P&O Ferries' announcement, Nautilus provided legal advice and industrial guidance to its sacked members, much of it concerning owed backdated pay and lost personal belongings. Officials and members took part in a series of hastily organised nationwide protests over the moves. The union helped to keep the issues in the public eye by organising a banner in support of P&O Ferries seafarers at a Liverpool home game, and creating a protest projection onto the white cliffs of Dover, as well as working with the ITF to make top-level representations to P&O Ferries' parent company, DP World, based in Dubai.

Detailed briefings were given to MPs, including opposition leader Keir Starmer, ahead of Parliamentary debates on the scandal. Barely a week after the seafarers had been sacked, Nautilus gave evidence to the House of Commons Transport Committee, drawing particular attention to the safety issues raised by P&O Ferries' actions – questioning the training and experience of replacement crews, their familiarity with the ships, and the risks of working on car decks. In the light of reports that the agency crews would be working on tours of duty of up to eight weeks, the union noted the 'plethora of evidence' about the risks of seafarer fatigue, and argued that flag states should withdraw their safe manning documentation for the ships until P&O Ferries management had submitted revised proposals to reflect the new operating patterns.

Mark Dickinson told MPs:

> In a safety-critical industry such as shipping, the importance of a competent, well-trained, experienced crew cannot be overstated. This is even more the case in a company such as P&O Ferries where, in addition to the risks that are present in all shipping operations, there exists the additional pressures inherent in operating vessels to extremely tight schedules, with rapid turnarounds in the busiest shipping lanes in the world.

With the company seeking to return the ships to service within a matter of days, the union also contacted the Maritime & Coastguard Agency (MCA) to call for full inspections of the vessels, with a special focus upon the suitability of the new crews. Nautilus warned: 'We consider that it is extremely unlikely that any company that has replaced its entire crew overnight would be able to demonstrate compliance with the mandatory requirements relating to crew training and familiarisation.'

The day after the union had appeared before the transport committee, the MCA detained the ferry *European Causeway* in Larne, Northern Ireland, when an inspection found a total of 31 safety deficiencies, including 'failures on crew familiarisation, vessel documentation and crew training'. Further detentions followed – including the *Pride of Kent* and *Spirit of Britain* – and yet more safety concerns were raised when *European Causeway* broke down and lost power in the Irish Sea barely a fortnight after it had returned to service.

The transport committee had given the P&O Ferries' CEO a tough time, one member opening proceedings by asking him: 'Are you in this mess because you don't know what you're doing, or are you just a shameless criminal?' But while Hebblethwaite admitted to unlawfully sacking staff without consulting with unions, he defended the move on the grounds that 'it was our assessment that the change was of such a magnitude that no union could possibly accept our proposal'. And, he added, he would do the same again, as it had been the only way to save the company.

P&O Ferries rejected calls from the unions and MPs for the seafarers to be reinstated and to return to the negotiating table. Asked about the pay of replacement crew members, Hebblethwaite (who at the time admitted that his annual salary was £325,000[16]) told the MPs the average would be around £5.50 an hour. 'This is an international seafaring model that is consistent with models throughout the globe and our competitors,' he argued.

However, one month after the new crews started work it was revealed that P&O Ferries was paying some of them what Nautilus branded the 'despicably low' basic wage of £3.94 per hour. The ITF said it had been approached by several seafarers working in Dover and Hull at a rate of $860 (£683) a month for a 40-hour working week. One contract for an AB seen by Nautilus ran for 17 weeks and required the crew member to work 12 hours a day, seven days a week. When overtime, leave and a subsistence allowance was included the rate of pay would rise to £5.10 an hour, based on an 84-hour working week – well below the then UK National Minimum Wage of £9.50 an hour.

However, while ministers had initially talked tough – with Prime Minister Boris Johnson telling Parliament 'We will take them to court, we will defend the rights of British workers … P&O Ferries plainly aren't going to get away with it' – they began, within a fortnight, to pull their punches, with Transport Secretary Grant Shapps admitting: 'The government are not in a position to take court action.'

Similarly, the then business secretary, Kwasi Kwarteng, had originally warned P&O Ferries that it could face an unlimited fine when he announced that he had asked the Insolvency Service to conduct an urgent investigation of the legality of the company's actions. He told the company that its failure to give the required notice of the redundancies 'is a criminal offence'. However, in August the government agency said that it had determined there was 'no realistic prospect of a conviction'.

Nautilus responded to the Insolvency Service's announcement with the

---

16 https://www.bbc.co.uk/news/business-61239415

statement: 'P&O Ferries has gotten away with it. There's no fine, there's no legal action, there's only words and hot air. What we're really after now is systemic change so this can never happen again.' The TUC also urged the government to 'urgently bring forward an Employment Bill to stop workers from being treated like disposable labour – and make sure what happened at P&O Ferries never happens again'.

By the end of March, ministers produced a nine-point plan which, Shapps claimed, would force P&O Ferries to 'fundamentally rethink their decision'. The package, he told MPs, would 'send a clear message to the maritime industry that we will not allow this to happen again. That where new laws are needed, we will create them. Where legal loopholes are cynically exploited, we will close them. And where employment rights are too weak, we will strengthen them'.

The proposals included plans to crack down on the enforcement of the NMW, where applicable, by UK ferry operators, and a review of the MCA's enforcement policies. There would also be new powers for harbour authorities to refuse access to UK ferry operators failing to pay NMW rates, as well as a new statutory code of practice to prevent 'fire and rehire' practices. The government also said that it would seek to create minimum wage 'corridors' between the UK and other countries.

While Nautilus gave a guarded welcome to the package, it noted that intervention on the NMW alone would neither stop P&O Ferries nor disincentivise other companies from sacking their workers. The TUC also warned that the package could prove worthless without adequate action to ensure that the rules were enforced. It told the government that there should be a framework agreement with unions at both ends of shipping routes between Britain and the EU to set minimum rates of pay, together with greater powers for HM Revenue & Customs inspectors to board ships to check whether companies are paying staff the minimum wage.

Noting that P&O Ferries had carefully calculated the penalty it might have to pay for failing to follow the requirements to consult its workers before making the job losses, and had factored that into the redundancy package, Nautilus argued that it set a very dangerous precedent: 'If you have deep enough pockets, you can pay your way out of complying with the law'.

Working with the RMT, Nautilus presented ministers with a Fair Ferries Strategy which would introduce legislation for an industry-wide national framework collective bargaining agreement. Covering all routes to and from UK ports, the agreement would be coupled with a certification approval process, to be enforced by the MCA. This would ensure that all ferry operators in the UK were required to work with social partners and apply, as a minimum, the agreed framework. This strategy was to be supported by an ongoing Fair Ferries Campaign to achieve a sustainable future for the sector, protect members' jobs, and secure quality long-term employment for UK-based seafarers.

Supporting its strategy, Nautilus published the results of a public opinion survey showing that almost two-thirds of the 2,000 respondents believed that P&O Ferries' CEO and directors should face prosecution for unlawfully dismissing their seafarers. Nearly 80 per cent considered that companies such as P&O Ferries should not be allowed to hire agency crews to replace sacked seafarers, and 85 per cent believed that seafarers working in the UK should have the same employment rights as shore-based staff.

The government pressed ahead with its plans, introducing the Seafarers' Wages Bill into Parliament in July 2022. The new legislation would empower harbour authorities (a) to request declarations from operators of international freight and passenger services to confirm that they paid seafarers a rate equivalent to the UK NMW, and (b) to refuse access to vessels that failed to do so. The harbour authorities would also be able to impose a surcharge on operators, as a deterrent to companies using cheap labour.

While welcoming the long-awaited action to enforce minimum wage requirements in the ferry sector, Nautilus pointed to a number of loopholes within the Bill, questioning whether the harbour authorities were the appropriate bodies to enforce the rules, given that many of them were run by the same companies that they would be policing. During debates on the proposals, many MPs backed the union's position, arguing that the measures failed to go nearly far enough and that the measures would do nothing to support permanence of employment, nor incentivise the use of domestically resident labour, nor address the appalling conditions imposed on agency workers. Concerns were also raised about a change from the original draft, in which 'frequent' visits to UK ports had been defined as 52 times a year, to a new threshold of 120 times per year, making it easier for unscrupulous companies to evade paying the NMW.[17]

The TUC also urged the government to go further, by ending the long-running legal confusion over whether in cases such as the P&O Ferries scandal unfairly dismissed seafarers were covered by British employment law. The Insolvency Service had cited a 'lack of legal clarity' as to whether the crews worked outside

---

17 The less rigorous criteria would enable some owners to adjust the schedule of port calls as a way to avoid the rules. SNP MP David Linden summed it up well: 'I am concerned that the Government have dismissed out of hand the unions' concerns over avoidance techniques. Port hopping, as we often refer to it, remains a genuine avoidance technique that becomes far easier to use the more frequently a vessel calls at a UK harbour. At 120 calls per year, it would be far easier for operators to make minor changes to scheduled port calls in order to avoid the legislation. A threshold of 52 calls, which was in the Government's original proposals, would be far tighter. It was changed only after consultation with industry, although the trade unions supported 52 calls.'

Great Britain as one of the key reasons why it had not pursued criminal charges against P&O Ferries.

On 7 February 2023 the Bill passed its third and final reading in the House of Commons. Mark Dickinson said:

> Whilst we are pleased to see the government pass primary legislation to ensure seafarers on vessels calling regularly at UK ports are paid at least the UK National Minimum Wage, this cannot be the sum total of government action. The government must close all the legal loopholes exposed by P&O Ferries' actions and ensure safe rostering patterns and crewing levels are included in a bilateral agreement with neighbouring countries. We look forward to continuing to work with government to ensure ambition will be met with action.'

In the same month the government also published its plans to deal with the 'fire and rehire' tactics which it had promised to tackle following the P&O Ferries débâcle. The proposals included a statutory code of practice which 'makes it explicitly clear to employers that they must not use threats of dismissal to pressurise employees into accepting new terms, and that they should have honest and open-minded discussions with their employees and representatives'.

The government stated that courts and employment tribunals would have the power to apply a 25 per cent uplift to an employee's compensation in certain circumstances if an employer was found not to comply with the statutory code. Nautilus noted that while the proposals would not prevent a repeat of the P&O Ferries scandal, they would make it a much costlier exercise for unscrupulous employers.

As the first anniversary of the sackings was marked, much had already been achieved by the union. However, it was clear that the government's actions were not nearly strong enough and that much still needed to be done. Mark Dickinson stressed that the government's response had failed to protect seafarers from similar summary dismissal in future, and that the legal loopholes which enabled P&O Ferries to act in the way it did had not been closed. While Nautilus supported the move to extend NMW coverage to seafarers regularly entering UK ports, he pointed out that it was not enough to address the wider issues which had been highlighted by the dispute, and much more was required to support sustainable employment and career opportunities for maritime professionals.

This would include the creation of a Seafarers' Welfare Charter, something the UK government had committed to creating following the actions of P&O Ferries. This charter could have a potentially significant positive impact on employment protections for maritime professionals beyond the ferry sector. However, the government chose to make that a voluntary document, so Nautilus's lobbying and campaigning continued, with the effect that the House of Commons Transport Select Committee, agreeing with the union's position, endorsed the creation of a mandatory charter.

A year on from the sackings, Nautilus could look back with pride on what it had achieved during and after the P&O Ferries crisis; it had overcome the usual public and political apathy about matters maritime and achieved significant political victories that had translated into changes in the law.

However, the Fair Ferries Campaign was destined to continue. Nautilus settled in for a long fight on behalf of UK seafarers – a fight to close the loopholes that had allowed the company to carry out its disgraceful coup against its own employees, and to guarantee a secure future for UK-based seafarers.

While the P&O Ferries débâcle may have served as a catalyst for some long-awaited, if limited, action to address seafarers' working conditions and to improve employment rights in the UK, it represented a major setback for the policy drive to reverse the decline in British shipping and seafaring. The company's actions raised significant concerns about the future of the Maritime 2050 programme, tarnishing the reputation of the industry and the efforts made to attract a new generation of skilled and committed British seafarers. Among the immediate casualties were 40 cadets who had been told to leave the ships and return home; Nautilus told the House of Commons transport committee that the sackings had sent out a 'message that British seafarers are expendable'. Even the former Conservative shipping minister, Sir John Hayes, pointed to the way in which P&O Ferries had undermined the aims of the Maritime Growth Study. 'It seems to me,' he told Parliament, 'that the fundamental point is that terms and conditions cannot be separated from wages. If we are going to make maritime careers attractive to people and build them such that they have the status they deserve, we really do have to include terms and conditions in our considerations.'

Quite what, if anything, P&O Ferries will have gained from its actions may take a long time to emerge. The company lost passenger and freight bookings at a key time of the year, as well as taking a huge public relations hit. In the long run its action has also caused incalculable damage to the image of the shipping industry and the seafaring profession. As one Nautilus International member reflected: 'I was sacked for doing my job – sacked for being a maritime professional. What sort of message does that send out?'

17 Where to now?

As we reflect on the actions of P&O Ferries it is evident that the drive towards social dumping has been a recurring challenge to Nautilus throughout its history. From the actions of BP in the 1980s to the actions of Irish Ferries in the mid-2000s, a consistent trend in attacks on the terms and conditions of maritime professionals runs parallel to the history of Nautilus and its predecessor unions.

Early in 2020 the union had to rise to the challenge of another crisis as a global health emergency demonstrated the strength of its ethos of internationalism and solidarity.

The Covid-19 pandemic plunged the world, and in particular the international shipping industry, into a profound crisis, creating severe problems for seafarers and presenting critical challenges to Nautilus. With important sectors such as cruise shipping, ferries, superyachts and the offshore energy industry hit hard, a very real threat to members' jobs and training rapidly emerged. The union pressed several governments over the plight of the thousands of seafarers who were unable to access the widespread and powerful support, such as the UK's Job Retention Scheme, given to other workers, and Nautilus also sought to minimise employers' moves to cut pay and conditions in response to the crisis.

The immediate impact of Covid-19 was followed by widescale health and welfare problems, as the lockdowns meant that those seafarers still at work were increasingly prevented from returning home on time, had their contracts extended, and were denied shore leave and medical care – while facing increased workloads, additional isolation, and yet more stress and fatigue than normal.

Nautilus rose to these multiple challenges, dealing with a torrent of individual and collective Covid-related cases, many involving members serving on ships where the disease had broken out. As the global total of seafarers stuck at sea soared to more than 250,000, the union played a core part in the industry's efforts to get the world's governments to recognise the key worker status of seafarers and to uphold their rights to repatriation. It lobbied for the creation of special vaccination centres, open to seafarers of all nationalities, to help ease the pressures caused by the pandemic, and it called for members to be given visa, border and quarantine exemptions to ensure that there were no unnecessary barriers to crew changes, repatriation, shore leave and medical attention.

Nautilus also successfully fought moves by a number of shipping companies to cut jobs, pay and conditions in response to the crisis. While employers in key sectors such as cruise shipping, ferries, large yachts, and the offshore oil and gas industry were seeking to amend collective bargaining agreements or lay members off, the union was developing strategies to resist compulsory redundancies and to ensure that proper consultation would take place before action.

In September 2020, seeking to ensure that lessons would be truly learned from such experiences, the union called for governments to undertake a comprehensive review of the global shipping industry and the resilience of supply lines. It said that serious attention should be paid to the way in which governments around the world were able to ignore conventions intended to protect the fundamental rights of seafarers during the pandemic.

In the spring of 2021 the union intensified its efforts to secure a better future for the industry by launching its Build Back Fairer campaign. This set out measures to prevent a return to the 'business as usual' scenario of a declining maritime sector and a race to the bottom both on seafarers' rights and on safety and environmental standards.

Noting that the pandemic had exacerbated many long-standing problems within the shipping industry, Nautilus called for permanent worldwide recognition of seafarers as key workers. It proposed action to improve global governance of the shipping industry, with a 'new era of accountability and transparency', and also highlighted the way in which so many important elements of global conventions on seafarers' rights had been quickly discarded as Covid spread throughout the world. Working through the ILO, Nautilus joined with other unions in pressing the UN to establish an inter-agency investigation into violations of the Maritime Labour Convention during the pandemic.

The Covid crisis had also shone the spotlight on the worrying and increasing evidence of mental welfare problems affecting seafarers. In the UK, the House of Commons transport committee endorsed evidence presented by Nautilus with a report concluding that 'welfare standards are inextricably linked to contractual terms and conditions' and calling on the government to take a lead by significantly exceeding the minimum standards set by the MLC, including the adoption of a mandatory seafarers' welfare charter. In the Netherlands, the union revealed research showing the negative impact of Covid on members' workloads and job satisfaction, and it raised these issues at a conference on maritime mental health organised by the European Transport Workers' Federation (ETF) in September 2022.

The Build Back Fairer campaign also sought to galvanise progress on the UK government's Maritime 2050 policy proposals. It urged ministers to take the 'unique opportunity' to reverse the decades-long decline in UK seafarer numbers by increasing the value of the SMarT training support scheme, requiring employers to guarantee a period of post-cadetship employment, and to tighten the tonnage tax scheme with a mandatory flag link and training commitments. Nautilus also pursued these objectives through its membership of the Maritime Skills Commission, established by the government to find ways to ensure that the sector's skills needs would be met, by better identifying future requirements and safeguarding a supply of talented new entrants. The commission did not take long to conclude that the continued quality of UK seafarer training was at risk of becoming outdated, and radical and rapid change was required to ensure that British seafarers had a decent chance of competing in global labour markets, through a secure supply of officers 'with differentiated leadership and technical skills'.

Build Back Fairer also tapped into the wider industry debate over the increasing impact of new technologies and pressure to radically reduce shipping's environmental impact. Early in 2018, as Norway led the charge to introduce autonomous shipping services and manufacturers such as Rolls-Royce unveiled detailed plans for 'smart' connected and data-centric systems to enable remote-controlled operations, Nautilus took the lead in formulating a policy that sought to prevent seafarers from being overlooked in the industry's apparent rush to embrace automation. The 21 unions in the Nautilus Federation worked together on a membership survey that assessed the views of maritime professionals on the rapid advances in shipboard technology and the prospect of crewless robo-ships. The resulting report recommended ways in which new systems and equipment could be used to improve safety and working conditions, ease workloads and administrative burdens, and improve predictive and preventive maintenance rather than simply being used to cut jobs.

Nautilus also contributed to the development of the top-level paper, *Mapping a Maritime Just Transition for Seafarers*, produced as part of the international shipping industry's response to the global climate emergency. The document had been commissioned by the Maritime Just Transition Task Force, formed at the UN's COP26 conference in Glasgow in 2021. It included a 10-point action plan to ensure that seafarers are reskilled to handle alternative fuels as part of the industry's moves to decarbonise operations, with an emphasis on strengthening global training standards and ensuring a health and safety-first approach.

Echoing these developments, Nautilus had also developed its 2030 Vision as a blueprint for the future. The policy document was based on work by the council to identify long-term financial, demographic, recruitment and organisational challenges for the union, and it was adopted at the 2019 General Meeting. It emphasised the need for agile responses to globalisation, automation and other trends, and set out ways in which Nautilus could continue adapting to meet the challenges of the future, including new ways of working and organising, new ways of campaigning and new ways of servicing members.

The 2030 Vision underscored the way in which the models of union organisation pioneered by Nautilus have provided an effective counterbalance to the fragmented and complex chains of ship ownership, management and operation, and the internationalised nature of members' employment. It commits the union to further cross-boundary cooperation with other like-minded organisations for maritime professionals as part of a strategy to ensure that 'the scale of the challenges faced by Nautilus is matched by the scale of its ambition'. The significance of that ambition had been highlighted nearly a decade earlier in an academic study – *Re-imagining Global Union Representation Under Globalisation* – published in 2013. This described the creation of Nautilus International as 'a unique and bold step in the renewal of trade union organisation' and one which set 'an important example to emulate as unions re-engineer their organising structures according to the emerging order'.

As the wider shipping industry faces up to the maritime implications of the fourth industrial revolution, Nautilus seeks to stress the continued importance of the 'human element' and the need to address the growing recognition of the mental health problems being stoked up by the many negative trends affecting seafarers. If owners are serious about attracting the highly qualified and committed workforce they need, the union challenges them to create a more humane working culture that eliminates the seemingly ever-present problems of excessive working hours, fatigue, stress and poor communications.

In its work to secure a more human-centred future for the shipping industry, Nautilus remains rooted in the core principles which had resulted in the creation of the MMSA. The need for what the founders described as 'a large and powerful body' to protect the interests of maritime professionals has remained as important as it ever was, with age-old issues such as pay, working conditions, health and safety, criminalisation, piracy and unfair competition as pertinent to the present day as they were back in 1854. Rightly proud of its past, and continuing to build on the far-seeing visions of its forerunners, the union retains its role as a critically important voice within an industry that remains an essential part of modern life.

The union has over its history evolved to keep pace with the change of industry and the constant fluctuations in the economic and political framework in which it operates, and where that evolution leads to next will always be into the most effective mechanism for improving the lives of maritime professionals. It is important to learn from the past in driving changes needed for the future; and in a very global industry it is a very global union that seems able to better serve the interests of those it represents.

The continued importance of the Nautilus Federation, the continued work with like-minded organisations, and the continued work matching pace with the curve of progress will deliver outcomes needed in the defence of jobs and skills, and the prospect of a fair maritime future for the people that work within the sector.

Challenging times lie in both directions from today. Looking back, Nautilus has demonstrated so clearly its ability to rise to meet these challenges, giving every confidence, therefore, that the future it faces, as challenging as it may seem, is a future that will be driven by embracing change and progress whilst defending the rights of those it represents.

As MNAOA General Secretary Doug Tennant told members back in 1969: 'I am convinced we can turn change to advantage. But this will only be possible with your determined support to ensure that out of increased productivity and efficiency you obtain your rightful share …'

Addenda

General secretaries of Nautilus International and predecessor unions

Mark Dickinson 2009 to the time of writing (est. 2009 Nautilus International by the merger of NUK and NNL)

Brian D. Orrell OBE, 1993–2009 (NUMAST and Nautilus UK)

Marcel van den Broek, Voorzitter, 2005 to the time of writing (FWZ and Nautilus NL)

Ed Sarton, Voorzitter, 1995–2005 (FWZ)

John Newman, 1989–1993 (NUMAST est. 1985, when MMSA/MNAOA and REOU merged)

Eric Nevin, 1974–1989 (MNAOA and NUMAST)

W.W.P. 'Bill' Lucas, 1975–1985 (MMSA) *

John W. Slater, 1971–1974 (MNAOA)

Douglas Tennant CBE, 1943–1971 (MNAOA, created in 1956 when MEA and NEOU merged)

William Coombs, 1935–1943 (NEOU est. 1935)

E. Grubb, MEA 19??–1956

W.G.D. Holloway, 1943–19??

David Bramah, MEA 1916–1943

William Marshall, MEU/MEA 1891–1916 (MEU est. 1887, changed name to MEA 1899)

Thomas Warren Moore, Imperial Merchant Service Guild, 1907–1936 (its amalgamation with MMSA)

John Grant Moore, Merchant Service Guild, 1893–1907

Radio Officers' Union

Kevin Murphy, 1968–1985 Radio and Electronic Officers' Union (REOU), est. 1968

Hugh O'Neill, 1949–1968

Harry J. Perkins, 1938–1949 Radio Officers' Union (ROU) est. 1937
T.J. O'Donnell, 1929–1938
E.R. Tuck, 1912–1929 Association of Wireless Telegraphists (AWT), est. 1912, became Association of Wireless and Cable Telegraphists (AWCT) in 1921

*MMSA secretaries

W.L.S. Harrison, 1956–1974
Alfred Wilson, 1933–1956
Thomas Scott, 1914–1933
C.P. Grylls, 1899–1914
J.J. Grylls, 1874–1899
Clarke Aspinall, 1865–1874
B.J. Thomson, 1857–1865

Notable figures

David Bramah

Elected as the general secretary of the Marine Engineers' Association in 1916, David Bramah was a passionate advocate of the work of his members, which he described as 'out of sight, out of mind'. After serving an apprenticeship at a locomotive works in Manchester, he joined White Star Line in 1898, rising to the rank of chief engineer before his appointment as secretary of the MEA's Liverpool branch in 1911. In five years in that post he was credited with recruiting more than 3,250 new members. He was also praised for giving 'valuable and practical' advice to the inquiry into the *Titanic*'s loss, and was awarded a CBE in 1920 in recognition of his work to help establish the National Maritime Board during the First World War.

Nick Bramley

Another architect of the development of Nautilus International was Nick Bramley. Born and educated in the UK, he moved to Switzerland in the 1980s and worked for a publishing firm before taking up a post with the chemical workers' union. After a decade with them, he moved to what was then the VHTL union, which merged to become the Unia general union in 2004, where he took responsibility for seafarers, Rhine boat crew and river workers.

A passionate defender of the interests of inland navigation workers around the world, Bramley served as president of both the International Transport Workers' Federation (ITF) and European Transport Workers' Federation (ETF) inland navigation sections, and was awarded the ITF's Gold Badge for distinguished service.

Marcel van den Broek

Born in The Hague in 1960, Marcel van den Broek started his nautical training at the age of 18. He studied for his deck officer qualifications at colleges in Flushing and Rotterdam, and served with Vroon for five years before coming ashore to work as a cargo surveyor in Rotterdam. He ran his own business in Ecuador for five years before returning to the Netherlands in 1999. He began working for Dutch union FWZ in May 2000, starting as an industrial officer. He was appointed president of the union in 2005 and became assistant and later deputy general secretary of Nautilus International when the new union was formed in 2009.

Mark Dickinson

The first Nautilus International general secretary, Mark Dickinson joined the union in January 2000. A former navigating officer, he served a cadetship with Bank Line, and worked at sea from 1978 to 1987 before going ashore to study at the University of Wales and the London School of Economics. He joined NUMAST after 12 years working for the ITF, where he led the successful mission to locate the wreck of the bulk carrier *Derbyshire* and oversaw the International Transport Workers' Federation (ITF) *Global Mariner* round-the-world voyage to highlight the 50th anniversary of the Flag of Convenience campaign.

Hijlke Hijlkema

With more than 41 years of working for the Dutch union FWZ, Hijlke Hijlkema possessed knowledge and experience described as vital in the creation of Nautilus. In his post-merger role as senior policy advisor, he was praised as being a 'rock' in helping to build a union fit for the future. He first went to sea in 1971 and served as a navigating officer in the Dutch deep-sea and coastal fleets before taking up a post with the FWZ in 1974. He served in a wide range of roles, including time as general secretary, in the accounts department, negotiating collective bargaining agreements and representing seafarers on the boards of four pension funds. He was awarded an ITF Gold Badge in 2014 to recognise his long service in support of seafarers.

Captain Charles Judkins

The commodore of the Cunard fleet, Captain Judkins, moved the very first motion at the 1857 meeting that established the MMSA, which he had helped to organise with local shipowner Ralph Brocklebank. During his 31 years of service with Cunard, Judkins served on some of its most prominent ships, including *Britannia*, *Persia* and its last ocean-going paddle steamer, *Scotia*. Captain Judkins was acclaimed as having 'never met with any accident' and being 'exceedingly popular with voyagers from both sides of the Atlantic'. He was a strong supporter of the Royal Naval Reserves, from its launch in 1859, and was appointed to the honorary rank of commander.

William Marshall

Born in Sunderland in 1853, William Marshall served as general secretary of the Marine Engineers' Union for 25 years after succeeding the first general secretary, Harry Moore, who had retired through ill health after 12 months in the post. Following an engineering apprenticeship, Marshall served on ships operating out of north-east England ports until he was elected MEU general secretary in May 1891. He was a member of the local marine board in London for 40 years, and served on the committee of the Seamen's National Insurance Society from its formation in 1912 until his death in 1933.

Peter McEwen

A key figure in the negotiations which led to the creation of Nautilus International, Peter McEwen joined the MNAOA in 1978 and served with the union until 2014, rising to the post of deputy general secretary. As secretary of the Nautilus Welfare Fund (NWF) for 15 years, he oversaw key programmes to expand and improve the union's welfare services, including the construction of the Trinity House Hub at Mariners' Park. As well as serving as chairman of the Merchant Navy Welfare Board, he was chair of the MNOPF for 15 years, secretary of the JW Slater Memorial Fund for 25 years, chair of the Seamen's Hospital Society, and a past trustee of Seafarers UK, the Mission to Seafarers and the Maritime Educational Foundation.

Captain John Grant Moore

Captain Moore was the founder of the Merchant Service Guild in February 1893. A Liverpool resident, he had served his apprenticeship sailing vessels out of Maryport, Cumberland, and at the early age of 21 gained his master's certificate and the command of a sailing ship. He went on to serve as master of most of the principal steamers in the Guion Line before retiring from the sea to establish a nautical academy in Liverpool, one of the first British educational establishments to teach nautical sciences. Then, after 'frequent and pressing representations made him by deputations of shipmasters and officers', Captain Moore agreed to establish the MSG in 1893. He served as secretary of the guild for 14 years and was succeeded by his son, Thomas Warren Moore, who had helped to establish the organisation.

Admiral Philip Nelson-Ward

On 31 December 1935 a headline in the *Daily News* proclaimed: 'ADMIRAL TO LEAD UNION'. Born in 1866, Admiral Philip Nelson-Ward was key to the launch of the Navigators' and Engineer Officers' Union. A descendant of Horatio Nelson, he first went to sea as a midshipman at the age of 13. Rising to the rank of captain in 1905, he became assistant hydrographer at the Admiralty in 1912 and in the following year was appointed the first director of navigation. Keenly interested in the Merchant Navy, especially after his involvement with North Sea convoys in the First World War, he was a close friend of Officers' (MN) Federation founder Captain William Coombs, and served as the organisation's president, producing a report which recommended the creation of the NEOU, concluding that 'masters and officers are regarded by many owners as casual labourers, dismissible at whim at the end of any voyage'.

Eric Nevin

Appointed MNAOA general secretary following the death of John Slater, Eric Nevin led the union during the drastic decline of British shipping in the 1970s and early 80s and oversaw the merger which created NUMAST in 1985. After training onboard HMS Conway and at Liverpool Technical College, he served at sea for 11 years with Alfred Holt, Blue Funnel and Glen Lines. He joined the MNAOA as assistant district secretary in Liverpool in 1959 and represented the union on the governing bodies of organisations including the MNOPF, MNWB, MNTB, HMS Conway, the London Nautical School, the Marine Society and the King George's Fund for Sailors.

Brian Orrell

Joining the MNAOA in 1973 as a Liverpool-based district official, Brian Orrell was appointed NUMAST general secretary in 1993 and stepped down from the post after securing the successful merger to create Nautilus International in 2009. Mr Orrell began his seagoing career as an engineer cadet in 1965 and served with Blue Funnel and Ocean Fleets before joining the union. As chair of the International Transport Workers' Federation (ITF) seafarers' section from 2000 to 2010, he led the global workers' side in top-level negotiations which resulted in the adoption of such key measures as the Maritime Labour Convention (MLC), the Fair Treatment Guidelines for Seafarers, the Seafarers' Identity Documents Convention.

Ed Sarton

As president of the FWZ, Ed Sarton played a pivotal role fostering the creation of Nautilus International with his clear and deep appreciation of the synergies between Dutch and British maritime professionals. After training at the Maritime Academy in Scheveningen, Mr Sarton first went to sea in 1966, serving as an apprentice mate with the Royal Nedlloyd Steam Ship Company (KNSM). During a decade of seagoing service, he qualified as a master mariner. Active in the union from an early age, Mr Sarton was appointed as an administrative assistant with the FWZ in February 1976. He worked in the union's Singapore office from 1977 to 1979 and subsequently led a lot of its work at the International Transport Workers' Federation (ITF), International Maritime Organization (IMO), International Labour Organization (ILO) and International Federation of Shipmasters' Associations (IFSMA). He retired from the union at the end of 2009 and died in 2013.

`John Slater`

The MNAOA Council decided to establish the JW Slater Memorial Fund in tribute to the union's general secretary who died following a fall at its head office in April 1974. Born in the Shetland Isles, Slater had first gone to sea as a deck boy, and went on to obtain a foreign-going master's certificate, serving with a number of companies including Ellerman & Papayanni Lines before joining the union in 1954. The Slater Fund honoured his life by helping to support ratings with the cost of studying for officer certification.

`Douglas Tennant`

The first general secretary of the MNAOA, Douglas Tennant had been one of the founder members of the NEOU in 1935, with membership No. 1. Born in Newcastle, he served an apprenticeship with Common Bros and obtained his master's certificate in 1930. He came ashore to work for the Navigators' & General Insurance Company in 1934, and was appointed national organiser of the NEOU in January 1936. He served as chairman of the International Transport Workers' Federation (ITF) seafarers' section between 1961 and 1971, and played a key role in the development of a number of International Labour Organization (ILO) conventions.

`E.R. Tuck`

The first general secretary of the Association of Wireless Telegraphists – which was to later become the Radio Officers' Union – was E.R. Tuck, who had been leader of the Postal Telegraph Clerks' Association until 1914. Tuck had managed to fill his AWT role on a part-time basis until its growth led to his appointment as full-time general secretary in 1918. The *Daily Herald* reported that his sudden death in office in 1929 had been 'received with great regret in the trade union movement'. He was succeeded by T.J. O'Donnell, who had been the AWT's marine secretary since 1920 – and who was quoted in the *Belfast Telegraph* in

February 1923 under the headline 'Listen in if you want long hair', reporting that 'hair experts' had found that 'electrical disturbances' from wireless sets were having a remarkable effect in stimulating the scalp. Mr O'Donnell stated: 'We have 7,200 men in this association, and I do not think there are a dozen bald men among them.'

Peter de Vries

Pieter de Vries was head of the Dutch seafarers' union CKO for 11 years, and did much to build constructive working relationships with the NEOU and MNAOA – much of this through his work in the International Transport Workers' Federation (ITF) and International Mercantile Marine Officers' Association (IMMOA). Born in 1897, he first went to sea at the age of 18. Between 1927 and 1931 he worked for the Amsterdam Chamber of Trade in the Dutch East Indies. In 1932 he became the assistant secretary of the Dutch Master Mariners' and Mates' Union, and held the post until 1942, when the Nazis dissolved all the Dutch trade unions. Following the war, he was elected as president of the Netherlands Seafarers' and Fishermen's Union, and in 1948 he was elected as IMMOA president. He also became prominent in the ITF, becoming the chair of its fishers' section. De Vries retired from CKO in 1958 and moved to London to become the ITF's director of regional affairs. He was elected ITF general secretary in 1960 and then, re-elected in 1962, served in the post until his retirement in 1965.

Recurring themes

1857: 'It was an extreme hardship, a gross injustice, that they [the commanders of the mercantile navy of this country] should be placed in the position in which they now are, whenever, owing to any casualty or to any circumstance, they should unfortunately be in the position of having to undergo a trial for any accident which may happen to the ship they command' – Charles Holland, speaking at the public meeting which resulted in the formation of the MMSA

1875: 'Where are our ships going? Since the 1st of January 1874, 875 British ships were transferred to foreign flags. This is very suggestive in the present state of legislation on shipping matters' – MMSA reporter

1875: 'Shipmasters and the income tax – this is an old and vexed question. The arguments in favour of the exemption of men whose time is almost wholly spent in earning their livelihood at sea are very numerous and weighty, especially when their long absence precludes them from exercising their social and political rights and privileges' – MMSA reporter

1876: 'While a sufficient supply of trained British seamen is of primary importance to shipowners, it is also a matter of vital concern to the whole nation. We are so dependent upon foreign countries for a large proportion of food that it is necessary to our national existence that we be supreme as a naval power' – MMSA reporter

1877: The annual MMSA report expresses concern about the 'unjust and increasingly contemptible system of punishing certificated masters and officers by heavy penalties for errors of judgment, by courts professedly sitting to investigate, and from whose decision the only appeal is the grace and favour of the Board of Trade'.

1891: 'We do not enter into antagonism with our employer the shipowner, but unless we combine and respect ourselves the shipowner cannot and will not respect us, and so will refuse to give us fair remuneration for our labour.' – Letter to the *Shields Daily Gazette*, Monday 15 September

1898: 'The value of membership never strikes one so forcibly as when troublous time arrive, as they are only too liable to do with those who follow the calling of the sea' – Imperial Merchant Service Guild annual report

1899: 'Some of our mercantile marine officers – such as those in the great steamship lines – have doubtless a fairly good time of it, a permanent position, decent pay, and exceedingly comfortable quarters. But for the majority the way in which they earn their livelihood is best with so many difficulties, the reward is so meagre, the penalties are so many, that it is little wonder that one finds few among them to say a good word for their profession' – *Merchant Service Guild Gazette*

1901: 'Courts of Inquiry from time to time attribute disasters to "a defective look out" but do they trouble to inquire whether this "defective look out" is the result of a pernicious two-watch system which wakes a man in the middle of his natural rest to take duty when keenness of judgement and vision are essential?' – *Merchant Service Guild Gazette*

1905: After the number of foreign seafarers employed on UK, Isle of Menand Channel Islands ships in home and foreign trades rose from 25,277 in 1888 to 40,396 in 1903, the Marine Engineers' Association wrote to the Board of Trade to request 'the prevention of aliens obtaining Board of Trade certificates'. In response, the board wrote that 'the number of foreigners holding certificates in the British mercantile marine is very small' and that 'it appears to the Board that no sufficient case has been made out for preventing aliens obtaining certificates, especially bearing in mind the number of engineers who have taken employment under foreigners'.

1906: 'The nation is not yet awakened to the fact that its existence, that its prosperity, is closely bound up with the prosperity and efficiency of her Merchant Navy, nor has it realised the deep debt of gratitude that it owes to its Merchant Seamen. But I think, and I think that I have a right to say, that there are signs that this apathy is being dispelled.' – Lord Muskerry, speaking to the Merchant Service Guild annual general meeting

1906: 'At present, where two watches only are in vogue, an unjustifiable physical strain is imposed upon Officers. Day after day they must put in at least fifteen or sixteen hours' work, and the only rest they can obtain is in short stretches of about three and a half hours' – Merchant Service Guild annual report

1907: 'Log-book "faking" is a very old story … but it is difficult to say whether the practice has grown any the less. When a man has the alternative of either "faking" his log-book or losing his bread and butter, he is not likely to choose the latter' – *IMSG Gazette*, July 1907

1911: 'It is noteworthy that popular enthusiasm concerns itself almost exclusively with the Royal Navy, while the Merchant Service remains a sort of Cinderella, neglected by Parliament (for it is not a political force), ill-paid, ill-fed, remaining now in a condition scarcely more tolerable than that of fifty years ago' – The Marine Engineers' Association, June 1911

1914: 'Shipping, like other industries, is coming under the control of combines with enormous capital whose main object is to provide dividends to those who provide the capital. Their motto is retrenchment of economy, and the economy is mainly to get the labour required at the cheapest possible rate. Those who have not got an active organisation to protect them are those who go to the wall' – Marine Engineers' Association

1934: The MMSA protests to the Board of Trade 'on the matter of the Euxine Shipping Company, registered in London, whose ships were manned entirely by aliens at absurd rates of pay'.

1936: 'The life aboard a very large number of British ships can only be described as a sordid existence, which is a disgrace to a nation claiming maritime supremacy and professing a high standard of civilisation' – NEOU general secretary Captain William Coombes

1936: 'The maxim "Unity is Strength" has been demonstrated time and time again, but for many years the officers of the Merchant Navy have ignored it and consequently the efforts to improve their pay and conditions have seriously been retarded.' The answer, said the MMSA reporter, was a single organisation for officers: 'The only argument which counts with employers is 100 per cent solid membership, and 100 per cent solid membership depends upon officers themselves.'

1936: The MMSA calls for the UK government to match other European countries by adopting a policy to protect domestic shipping and promote the employment of British seafarers. It pointed out that cargo preference policies meant that 90 per cent of cargo liner traffic between the UK and Denmark was being carried on Danish vessels, and that no British ships were carrying coal between the UK and France, and also that Germany and Sweden were protecting their vessels in similar ways.

1936: 'For too long the officers of the merchant marine have served at sea in dread of the time when they would be considered too old and, like the ships they staffed, be scrapped without any further regard' – Marine Engineers' Association

1937   In January the master of SS *Vanduara* was arrested by the Turkish authorities following a collision. Although he was subsequently absolved of all blame, he was not released until 15 February. The NEOU stated at the time: 'This incident again emphasises the need for international agreement under which ships' officers shall be answerable in cases if this kind only to the courts of the flag under which they serve.'

1937:   Motion to the first AGM of the NEOU warned that 'the need for amelioration of officers' hours of duty is urgent and if not met may have serious repercussions on the Service'.

1937:   PQ to the president of the Board of Trade asking about a collision between the British tanker *Helka* and the German liner *Pretoria*. The president, Oliver Stanley, confirmed that the only British seafarer on the *Helka* was the wireless operator, but added: 'Legislation requiring the universal employment of British officers and men in United Kingdom ships would not be likely to increase the employment of British officers and seamen but would probably lead to the transfer of some ships from the register.'

1945:   NEOU members call for membership of the union to be made compulsory: 'It is realised that full and complete effectiveness shall be obtained from their union only if the union is 100 per cent representative and that benefits to be derived from the union's activities warrant the duties of membership to be equally distributed.'

1950:   'Unless employment in the Merchant Navy is maintained on a basis which will provide a certain measure of security with a remuneration comparable at least with many shore occupations, the youth of our country – however strong the call of the sea may be – will look In other directions for a career and Britain will sink to the level of a third-rate power' – NEOU annual report

1954:   In a section on the exodus of ships to flags from countries with little or no maritime tradition, the NEOU annual report warned: 'The threat to the conditions of service of those sailing in ships of the bona fide maritime nations presented by this vast unlimited and continually expanding mass of tonnage is a very real one, potentially capable of inflicting incalculable hardship on seafarers the world over should there be a world recession of trade.'

1957:   The MMSA annual report complained about the 'irksome restrictions' experienced by seafarers seeking short leave in foreign ports as a consequence of 'the growth of extreme nationalism all over the world'. It backed proposals for an internationally recognised Seafarer's Identity Card, noting that 'the possession of such a card might well lead to a more understanding attitude towards foreign seafarers by officials in ports abroad'.

1957:   'I suggest that in future one of the planks in the platform of the MMSA should be to draw the attention of the British public to the fact that it relies more on its ships than on any other public service. It was learned in the First World War and we have learned it since ... In time of emergency we cannot rely on tonnage that is flying these flags of convenience.' – Captain George Ayre, MMSA president

1960:   'There is a highway around Britain – it gets bumpy at times, but it does not require repairing – and if we are to have an integrated transport system there must be a proper place within it (after all, we are an island) for coastwise shipping to be coordinated with other forms of transport.' – MNAOA General Secretary Douglas Tennant, in a speech to the TUC

1961:   'Shipowners are now required to compete for first-class personnel with professions and industries ashore. They have got to realise that a seafaring life sacrifices home life – it is a life served under trying and rapidly changing climatic conditions, it is a life that subjects personal considerations to sailing schedules, and it is a life involving hazards, and frequently long and irregular hours of duty. These disadvantages have got to be equated with the advantages of home life if ships are going to be sufficiently and efficiently manned.' – MNAOA General Secretary Douglas Tennant, opening the 1961 MNAOA General Meeting

1962: The MNAOA protests to the government after some fees for certificate of competency examinations are doubled or trebled following the repeal of legislation stipulating that seafarers should pay a maximum of 50 per cent of the costs.

1962: The MNAOA calls for talks with the Ministry of Transport over increasing concerns about the number of foreign seafarers being employed on UK ships.

1963: 'While the fully automated ship may be technically possible, it is still wishful thinking for many practical reasons at present … In the future, though it may be some way off, fewer people may be needed – but they will require different training and higher qualifications to handle complex electronic devices and safety equipment. The shipowners must not assume that by reducing crews as a result of scientific developments all the increased profits will be theirs. Seafarers must also share by way of substantially higher wages and better conditions.' – MNAOA General Secretary Douglas Tennant, speaking at the 1963 General Meeting

1967: Speaking in support of a General Meeting motion condemning excessive hours of work, one MNAOA member asked: 'Are we to have a major disaster before something is done?'

1974: 'We want to see the present income tax legislation for seafarers amended … If amendments were made in our favour, British officers of high calibre would tend to stay at sea longer and more men would be attracted into the industry, resulting in obvious benefits to the shipowner.' – Letter to *The Telegraph*, May 1974

2004: 'Young people today have so many more choices than we used to have. When I started, you did seven-month trips, even 13-month trips. We had to put ourselves through college, and were pretty much financially dependent on the next job. Today, thanks to the changed dynamic of the industry and action from organisations like NUMAST, companies pay towards training, and cadets and officers are on and off quite rapidly.' – Cunard Line Commodore Ron Warwick, interviewed by *The Telegraph*

2004: 'It can only be a matter of time before fatigue does result in major loss of life and major pollution, and it is shameful that it will apparently have to take such an incident before any substantive action is taken to ensure that vessels are properly manned in order to meet the requirements of their trade' – NUMAST national secretary Allan Graveson, commenting on a Marine Accident Investigation study showing that 60 ships had run aground around the UK coast over the past decade as a results of watchkeepers falling asleep or becoming incapacitated.

What has the union ever done for us?

1859: MMSA founded the Merchant Navy Cadet School onboard HMS *Conway* – an institution that it administered until 1968 and continued to provide education and training until 1974.

1879: MMSA helped to secure the right of appeal for shipmasters and officers involved in Board of Trade inquiries, opened homes for retired seafarers, and set up a welfare fund for aged seafarers.

1892: Improvements in dietary scales on British ships.

1894: Engineers formally recognised as officers, and engineers included as members of local marine boards.

1896: Board of Trade inquiry into manning recommended that certificate requirements for masters and mates be extended to coastal ships – finally agreed in 1911, together with the inclusion of certified engineers, following pressure from unions.

1897: MEU introduces a non-contributory accidental death payment scheme.

1905: MEA inaugurates its central benevolent Fund, providing support to members and their dependents 'in distress'.

1906: Following representations to the Board of Trade, 'the Societies representing Officers and seamen' secure an agreement that seafarers should have the right to call in an official of the Society to which they belonged in any case of dispute arising at the time of paying off.

1906: Merchant Service Guild secures improvements in salvage awards for deck officers following a decade of campaigning on the issue.

1907: Seafarers included in the provisions of the Workmen's Compensation Acts.

1907: Engineers given representation on casualty inquiries.

1908: Agreement on facilities for absent seafarers to vote in Parliamentary elections.

1912: First national agreement on pay scales.

1912: Following representations by organisations including the IMSG and the MEA, the government established the Seamen's National Insurance Society to administer NI contributions and payments for British seafarers.

1915: Admiralty agreement to pay war risk payments and up to 15 days of wages to crew and the fare home after their ship was sunk.

1916: A deputation of seafarers' organisations made representations to the Admiralty and the Board of Trade on the need for a standard uniform for masters and officers in the British mercantile marine: legislation was introduced in 1919.

1919: International Labour Organization agreement on special maritime sessions to consider 'the very special questions concerning the minimum standards to be accorded to seamen'..

1920: Association of Wireless Telegraphists secures a pay increase valued at 156 per cent.

1924: The MEA introduces a scheme of compensation for members in the event of suspension or cancellation of their certificate of competency.

1925: The Merchant Shipping Act established the principle of shipwreck pay, replacing the practice under which pay ceased with the loss of a vessel with an entitlement to pay for a maximum of two months after the casualty while a seafarer remained unemployed.

1930: A deputation of seafarers' organisations to the Railway Clearing House secured agreement on reduced fares (three-quarters of the normal rate) for officers and men of the mercantile marine travelling on leave in the UK.

1931: A petition from the Mercantile Marine Service Association and the Imperial Merchant Services Guild, signed by 8,729 navigating officers, was presented to Parliament. It called for the UK not to ratify Article 41 of the International Convention for the Safety of Life at Sea 1929, on the grounds that 'it would involve grave danger of catastrophe at sea'.

1932: The Watch Ashore was established.

1934: The IMSG obtains an important ruling that MN officers serving overseas for long periods 'should not be chargeable for income tax in respect their pay for any years which they may held not to be residents in the United Kingdom'.

1934: The Officers' Federation secures an £800 payment from the Portuguese government for a British ship's officer who was wrongfully imprisoned for 10 months in Portuguese West Africa.

1935: Central Board for the Training of Merchant Navy Officers established.

1936: The MEA and MMSA win a long campaign for members to have the right to unemployment insurance benefits when attending college to study for certificates.

1936: The Officers' Federation helps to secure the release of Captain Alexander Kane after he was sentenced to three years imprisonment by a Spanish court for 'forcibly resisting arrest' when he tried to break up a street fight ashore.

1936: The MMSA and the IMSG secure the agreement of the Ministry of Labour that officers will be able to draw unemployment benefit whilst attending courses to qualify for a Board of Trade certificate.

1937: John Davies Memorial Infirmary is opened at Mariners' Park.

1938: The MNOPF was established.

1939–1945: NEOU representations help to secure an agreement that wartime salvage awards should be free of income tax.

1940: Unions negotiate an agreement at the NMB which establishes for the first time that compensation should be paid to seafarers who lost their personal effects as a consequence of their vessel becoming a total loss 'by marine peril'.

1941: NEOU secures first agreement covering officers' hours of duty.

1943: Government inquiry recommends the creation of a Merchant Navy Welfare Board, composed of equal numbers of seafarer and shipowner representatives, to oversee the provision of suitable accommodation and recreational facilities for visiting seamen.

1947: Talks on British Seafarers' Charter, developed by the NEOU, result in an agreement which secures the withdrawal of shipowners' proposals to cut post-war pay by £7 a month.

1947: NEOU representations result in an agreement to almost double the wages of apprentices and cadets and, for the first time, compensation for officers working Sundays at sea.

1948: NEOU conference agrees to begin campaign for senior officers to be allowed to have their wives with them for at least six months in each two-year contract.

1952: Vigorous objections by the NEOU result in a decision to drop plans to withdraw concessionary rail fares for seafarers travelling to and from their ships.

1959: The MNAOA's income tax department reported that it had saved or recovered about £500,000 for members since the end of the war.

1960: The MNAOA claims success in ending the abuse of regulations for the carriage of British officers, with a new Merchant Shipping Bill extending the requirement for all British foreign-going and home trade passenger ships to 'carry certain officers holding statutory certificates of competency'.

1961: The International Labour Organization discusses proposals, which emanated from a motion at the MNAOA's 1957 General Meeting, for the Crew Accommodation Convention to be amended to make the installation of air conditioning compulsory in all new ships and in existing ships where practicable.

1962: Following representations by the MNAOA after accidents in which officers were injured when wheelhouse windows shattered, the Ministry of Transport introduces new recommendations for the use of solid or laminated toughened glass.

1962: On the 50th anniversary of the *Titanic* disaster, the MMSA launches a campaign to clear the name of Captain Stanley Lord – arguing that he had been the victim of the 'grossest miscarriage of justice' in being accused of failing to go to the aid of the sinking liner.

1965: The MMSA continued its campaign to clear the name of its member Captain Stanley Lord, presenting a petition to the Board of Trade calling for a reopening of the section of the inquiry into the loss of the *Titanic* which held that his ship ignored the liner's distress signals.

1967: Following a long campaign by the MNAOA, a Private Member's Bill introduced into the House of Commons by former MN officer and Labour MP Eric Ogden, ended the anomaly under which UK ships were able to leave foreign ports without the certificated officers specified in the Merchant Shipping Acts.

1970: MMSA's campaign to clear Captain Stanley Lord secures a new provision in the Merchant Shipping Act to ensure that no similar case could ensure without the right of appeal after censure by a court of inquiry.

1972: MNAOA agreement with British Shipping Federation secures promise from owners to 'work towards arrangements under which officers would receive leave on the basis of one day leave for every two days worked'.

1974: Discussions with DTI on certification and manning of oil rig supply vessels, as well as a review of minimum safe manning standards for small vessels, under 350dwt, in the home trades following the report on the abandonment of the cargo ship *Festivity* in the North Sea in November 1971.

1974: MNAOA establishes the JW Slater Fund, following the sudden death of general secretary John Slater in April. The Fund sought to support ratings studying to become officers and has gone on to provide scholarships to well over 1,000 seafarers seeking their first certificates.

1976: MNAOA negotiations establish one-on/one-off leave entitlement for officers serving on offshore supply vessels.

1976: MNAOA inaugurates the John William Slater Memorial Fund, in honour of the late general secretary, to provide financial support for ratings studying towards an officer's certificate of competency.

1977: Special income tax arrangements for seafarers were introduced following a working party established by the Inland Revenue, upon which the MNAOA was represented. The subsequent Finance Act introduced a 25 per cent overseas earnings deduction for those working abroad for 30 days or more, and 100 per cent in certain circumstances.

1977: MNAOA resists attempts to reduce standards during discussions with the Department of Trade and shipowners on the development of a new certificate of competency structure and officer

1977: The Secretary of State for Health declares that the Dreadnought Seamen's Hospital in Greenwich should remain open following a MNAOA campaign (including a 23,200-signature petition delivered to Downing Street) to reverse a health authority decision to close it.

manning levels. The union also secured transitional arrangements to protect officers successfully serving in posts where certification requirements were being introduced.

1978: Following representations by the MNAOA and consultations with the industry, the government introduces a code of practice to limit noise levels on ships.

1979: MNAOA established the Victoria Drummond Award, in memory of the first British woman to serve as a chief engineer and to honour the achievements of other female members.

1980: Strike by MNAOA members serving on Lowestoft trawlers secures an increase in guaranteed sea pay for masters and mates, as well as a promise to formally recognise the union.

1981: NUMAST launches the Victoria Drummond Award, commemorating the first woman to serve as a chief engineer officer and to promote the achievements of women members.

1984: Protests by the MNAOA over new medical standards and appeal procedures result in the creation of a review committee which recommends amendments that address the union's objections.

1986: NUMAST launches a personal pension plan for members serving with foreign flag companies or employers with no company schemes.

1987: Following warnings by the MNAOA about the growing shortage of certificated UK officers, the Secretary of State for Transport announces plans to introduce a system of government assistance for training seafarers.

1988: NUMAST protests help to secure the partial restoration of some of the special income tax concessions for British seafarers serving outside the UK for extended periods.

1989: NUMAST persuades government to grant exemptions from poll tax for seafarers out of the UK for six months or more each year.

1989: Industrial action by NUMAST members serving with Caledonian MacBrayne secures an 8 per cent pay increase to compensate for extra workloads arising from new summer schedules.

1990: Three NUMAST members, legally represented by the union, are cleared of manslaughter charges arising from the *Herald of Free Enterprise* disaster. 'We couldn't have done it without NUMAST,' said Captain David Lewry, the ship's master. 'The support from the union has been fantastic and if anyone at sea is wondering whether or not to join the union, they should take note of this.'

1991: NUMAST's long-running lobbying leads to the introduction, in the Finance Act, of the '183-day rule' to widen seafarers' eligibility for income tax rebates for work overseas.

1994: Years of campaigning by the MNAOA and NUMAST finally pays off when the government agrees that engineers suffering from hearing damage as a result of engine-room noise are eligible for industrial injuries disablement benefit.

1996: Following protests by NUMAST, the Inland Revenue relaxes its definition of a 'ship', ensuring that members serving on vessels such as FPSOs (floating production storage and offloading units) can continue to claim income tax concessions.

1996: NUMAST Personal Pension Plan is launched, providing a contributory scheme for members serving with foreign companies or employers refusing to pay into occupational schemes such as the MNOPF.

1998: NUMAST participation in national and international working groups assessing 'one-man bridge operations' helps to retain the requirement for an extra lookout to be posted in the hours of darkness.

1998: NUMAST protests help to ensure that seafarers income tax concessions are protected from a Budget decision to abolish the general foreign earnings deductions exemptions.

1999: an initiative developed by NUMAST and South Tyneside College results in the launch of the first training course for electro-technical officer cadets.

1999: NUMAST made a successful court challenge to a 1998 Budget decision which had prevented seafarers serving on vessels classed as offshore installations from claiming income tax concessions.

2000: NUMAST successfully campaigns against BP's plans to replace 17 North Sea emergency response and rescue vessels with six Super Puma helicopters.

2000: A second inquiry into the loss of the bulk carrier *Derbyshire* is launched in response to representations by NUMAST and the RMT following the successful ITF mission to locate the wreck site.

2001: NUMAST launches guidelines to combat bullying and harassment at sea, jointly developed with the UK Chamber of Shipping. The policies were subsequently adopted at European and international levels.

2001: NUMAST wins a landmark High Court ruling, with judges upholding a case brought by the union on behalf of three members working on jack-up rigs who argued that they should be classed as seafarers under Inland Revenue regulations for eligibility to foreign earnings income tax concessions.

2002: NUMAST opens the 32-bed Mariners' Park Care Home, providing nursing, residential care and short-stay/respite facilities.

2003: Following a NUMAST campaign against cuts in fire service cover for ships and offshore installations, the UK government announces a new national strategy for regional provision, centred upon brigades with specialist expertise.

2003: NUMAST and the Chamber of Shipping secure a U-turn by the UK government on plans to change the national insurance rules for seafarers on offshore contracts.

2005: NUMAST leads the seafarers' group in joint IMO/ILO talks to develop international guidelines for the fair treatment of seafarers following maritime accidents.

2006: NUMAST leads the seafarers' group in the negotiations to conclude the agreement on the ILO Maritime Labour Convention, ratified by the Netherlands and Switzerland in 2011 and by the UK in 2013. Nautilus played a key role in work on subsequent amendments to the convention (in 2014, 2016, 2018 and 2022) with general secretary Mark Dickinson elected as seafarers' spokesperson at the ILO in 2018.

2007: UK government announces plans to close the loopholes in the Race Relations Act which enabled shipowners to pay different rates to foreign seafarers.

2009: Nautilus secures a judicial review of controversial of controversial HM Revenue & Customs rules that would have stopped many members in the offshore sector qualifying for seafarers' income tax concessions.

2009: Following a two-week crown court trial, a shipmaster member, represented by the Union, is cleared of causing the deaths of three colleagues who entered an oxygen-deficient compartment onboard the vessel.

2010: A week-long IMO diplomatic conference in Manila adopts revisions to the Standards of Training Certification & Watchkeeping Convention, marking success for the union's long-running efforts to secure formal recognition of the role of the electro-technical officer as a certificated officer.

2010: After Nautilus reveals the extensive use of asbestos on newly built ships, the IMO backs proposals developed by the union and the Dutch government for addressing the problem and ensuring compliance with SOLAS Convention regulations banning its use.

2011: Nautilus announces a £4 million Trinity House Hub project to provide new residential and community facilities at Mariners' Park.

2011: The Equality Act (Work on Ships and Hovercraft) Regulations came into effect, prohibiting differential pay rates among EU nationals and seafarers from other designated states serving on UK register.

2011: Nautilus International's Swiss branch is created.

2012: Nautilus submits three papers to the IMO setting out proposals for improving the design and construction, training and crewing, fire-fighting and evacuation of passenger ships.

2012: The European Commission-backed Project Horizon study – in which Nautilus was a core participant – produces definitive evidence of the dangers and scale of seafarer fatigue, as well as developing a fatigue management toolkit to reduce the risks.

2014: HRH the Princess Royal opens the £4.1 million Trinity House Hub at Mariners' Park, providing 18 new apartments and community facilities for retired seafarers and their partners.

2014: Nautilus, ever vigilant on seafarers' income tax concessions (SED), secures important clarifications on this important element of the UK government's permitted state aid for the shipping industry.

2015: Long-running Nautilus demands for the government to adopt a bold strategy for the shipping industry leads to the Maritime Growth Study and a report by Lord Mountevans, setting out 18 recommendations for safeguarding the sector's future.

2015: Following extensive lobbying by Nautilus International, the European Social Partners' Agreement on Working Time in Inland Waterways Transport is signed, regulating working hours and setting limits on time on board.

2016: Nautilus sets out the case for the UK to remain a member of the EU in the face of the referendum and maintains the integrity of the One Union following the 'Brexit' vote, backed by the launch of a Charter for Jobs as its response to the 'benefits of Brexit'.

2017: HRH The Earl of Wessex opens the Seafarers' UK Centenary Wing, adding 22 new apartments to the Trinity House Hub facilities at Mariners' Park.

2018: Nautilus helps to secure government agreement to double the SMarT funding for UK seafarer training, together with commitments from leading shipowners to increase the annual cadet intake from 750 to 1,200.

2018: A new government–industry strategy, Maritime 2050, is launched, with government promises to ensure the UK remains a global leader in such areas as seafarer skills, maritime trade, and technology.

2018: Nautilus becomes a member of the industry umbrella group Maritime UK, and general secretary Mark Dickinson is appointed as a member of its national council.

2019: The Nautilus International General Meeting adopts the 2030 Vision to achieve financial sustainability. The bold programme identifies the many risks and challenges the union faces as well as its opportunities to evolve and grow, and to expand the support it provides to members.

2020: Nautilus general secretary Mark Dickinson is appointed to the Maritime Skills Commission, created by the government to deliver the 'people' chapter of the Maritime 2050 strategy. One of the commission's first tasks – to carry out a review of seafarer cadet training – leads to the launch of the Cadet Training and Modernisation Programme.

2020: Nautilus responds to the challenges of the Covid-19 pandemic to secure key worker status for its members and extended support for those who faced numerous challenges to continue to work, to access medical care and welfare support aboard, to secure vaccinations, and to continue to study and move freely despite severe restrictions.

2020: Following an extensive campaign by Nautilus, the government extends the UK National Minimum Wage to all seafarers in UK waters.

2020: Work begins on a project to redevelop the Gibson House site at Mariners' Park, creating 26 new apartments for retired seafarers and their dependents.

2021: Nautilus submits a report to the UK maritime minister demanding that the government's Build Back Better post-Covid recovery strategy is based on fairness for all workers.

2021: The Nautilus Caseworker Service recovers a record £1.32 million in benefits and grants for members in need.

2022: Reaping the rewards of its investment in strategic campaigning, Nautilus launches a highly effective campaign to highlight the unlawful actions of P&O Ferries in dismissing its entire UK seagoing workforce – which leads to widespread public, trade union and all-party political condemnation of the company's actions. In response, the government adopts a 'nine-point plan' to address seafarers' welfare.

2022: The union's head office is relocated to Nautilus House, Mariners' Park, in Merseyside, the historic home and effective birthplace of the oldest member of its family tree – the Mercantile Marine Service Association (MMSA), established in 1857.

2022: Nautilus secures amendments to the UK's Borders and Nationalities Bill, to avoid the risk of ships' officers being criminalised for recovering persons in distress at sea.

2023: Nautilus briefs MPs and ministers ahead of the introduction of the Seafarers' Wages Act, which introduces new obligations on ports to check that seafarers' wages are at least the UK National Minimum Wage if a vessel enters a UK port 120 times or more per annum.

2023: The UK government also introduces a Seafarers' Charter, presenting a set of voluntary standards to protect seafarer employment and welfare. Nautilus continues to call for its provisions to be made mandatory.

2023: Work starts at Mariners' Park on a new development involving the construction of 27 two-bed apartments for retired seafarers and their dependents, and a new office for Nautilus facilities, in the first collaboration between the union and the Nautilus Welfare Funds charity.

List of abbreviations, initialisms and acronyms

AB	Able seaman/able-bodied seaman
ACL	Atlantic Container Line
ACT	ACT Shipping, Mauritania
AGM	Annual General Meeting
ANZB	Algemene Nederlandse Zeemansbond (General Dutch Sailors' Association)
AVZ	General Association of Seafarers
AWCT	Association of Wireless and Cable Telegraphists
AWT	Association of Wireless Telegraphists (in 1921 became part of the AWCT)
BALPA	British Airline Pilots' Association
BGM	Biennial General Meeting
BMSL	British Merchant Service League
BP	British Petroleum (in 2001 became Beyond Petroleum)
CBA	Collective bargaining agreement
CBE	Commander of the British Empire
CBT	Centrale Bond van Transportarbeiders (Central Association of Transport Workers)
CCNR	Central Commission for the Navigation of the Rhine
CEC	Certificate of Equivalent Competency
CEO	Chief Executive Officer
CKO	Centrale van Koopvaardij-Officers
CKV	Dutch Seafarers' and Fishermen's Union
DFDS	Det Forenede Dampskibs-Selskab
DTI	Department of Trade and Industry
EC	European Communities (also European Commission, not in this book)
ETF	European Transport Workers' Federation
EU	European Union

FNV	Federatie Nederlandse Vakbeweging (Dutch Trade Union Federation)
FoC(s)	Flag(s) of convenience
FPSO	Floating production storage and offloading unit
FWZ	Federatie van Werknemers in de Zeevaart (Seafarers' Federation)
GCBS	General Council of British Shipping
GMDSS	Global Maritime Distress & Safety System
HAL	Holland-America Line
HM	Her Majesty/His Majesty
HQ	Headquarters
HTV	Gewerkschaft Handel, Transport, Verkeh (German Transport Workers' Union)
IBF	International Bargaining Forum
IFSMA	International Federation of Shipmasters' Associations
ILF	International Labour Federation
ILO	International Labour Organization
IMCO	Inter-Governmental Maritime Consultative Organization
IMEC	International Maritime Employers' Committee (in 2012 became International Maritime Employers' Council)
IMMOA	International Mercantile Marine Officers' Association
IMO	International Maritime Organization
IMSG	Imperial Merchant Service Guild
IOF	International Officers' Federation
ISF	International Seafarers' Federation
ISWAN	International Seafarers' Welfare and Assistance Network
ITF	International Transport Workers' Federation
JASON	Joint Assistance and Support Network
JMC	Joint Maritime Commission
JNG	Joint Negotiating Group
KBV	Nederlandse Katholieke Bond van Vervoerspersoneel (Dutch Catholic Union of Transport Personnel
KNSM	Koninklijke Nederlandse Stoomboot-Maatschappij (Royal Dutch Steamboat Company)
KTA	Kriegstechnische Abteilung (Swiss War Office)
KVNR	Koninklijke Vereniging van Nederlands Reders (Royal Association of Netherlands Shipowners)
LGBT+	Lesbian, gay, bisexual, transgender, intersex, queer/questioning, asexual and more
LGV	Lebens- und Genussmittelarbeiterverband (Swiss union for food, drink and tobacco workers)
MBE	Member of the British Empire

MCA	Maritime & Coastguard Agency
m dwt	millions: deadweight tonnage
m gt	millions: gross tonnage
MEA	Marine Engineers' Association
MEU	Marine Engineers' Union (in 1899 became the MEA)
MILAG	Marine Internierten Lager
MLC	Maritime Labour Convention
MMSA	Mercantile Marine Service Association
MN	Merchant Navy
MNAOA	Merchant Navy & Airline Officers' Association
MNOPF	Merchant Navy Officers' Pension Fund
MP	Member of Parliament
MSG	Merchant Service Guild
N&G	Navigators & General Insurance Company
NAS	National Labour Secretariat
NASFU	National Amalgamated Sailors and Firemen's Union (became the NUS)
NEOU	Navigators & Engineer Officers' Union
NL	Nederland/Netherlands
NMB	National Maritime Board
NMW	National Minimum Wage
NNL	Nautilus Nederland
NSFU	National Sailors' & Firemen's Union
NUK	Nautilus UK
NUMAST	National Union of Marine, Aviation and Shipping Transport Officers (in 2006 became Nautilus)
NUMM	National Union of Masters and Mates
NUS	National Union of Seamen (in 1990 became part of the RMT: National Union of Rail, Maritime and Transport Workers)
NVV	Nederlandsch Verbond van Vakvereenigingen (Transport Workers' Union)
NWF	Nautilus Welfare Fund
OCL	Overseas Containers Limited
ONC	Ordinary National Certificate
OND	Ordinary National Diploma
P&O	Peninsular & Oriental
Panlibhonco	Panamanian, Liberian, Honduran and Costa Rican
PM	Prime minister
PoW(s)	Prisoner(s) of war
REOU	Radio and Electronic Officers' Union

RMT	National Union of Rail, Maritime and Transport Workers
RO(s)	Radio officer(s)
ROU	Radio Officers' Union (in 1967 became the REOU)
SJC	Seafarers Joint Council
SMarT	Support for Maritime Training
SOLAS	Safety of Life at Sea
SOU	Shipmasters' and Officers' Union
SFr	Swiss francs
SSG	Swiss Shipping Company
STCW	Standards of Training, Certification and Watchkeeping for Seafarers
TAZ	Seafarers' Labour Market Taskforce
TSSA	Transport Salaried Staffs Association
TUC	Trades Union Congress
UK	United Kingdom
US	United States
VHT	Verband der Handels- und Transportarbeiter ([Swiss] Commercial and Transport Workers' Association)
VHTL	Verband der Handels-, Transport- & Lebensmittelarbeiter der Schweiz (Swiss Commerce, Transport & Food Workers' Association)
VKO	[Dutch] Association of Captains and Officers for Merchant Shipping
VNKO	Association of Dutch Merchant Marine Officers